Homeschooling at the Speed of Life is overflowing with wisdom and practical ideas. You'll be encouraged and motivated to get your life organized so that homeschooling can be a joy rather than one more burden. Even better, Marilyn provides instructions, lists, and forms in the book and its companion CD so you can get started immediately!

—Cathy Duffy

Author of *100 Top Picks for Homeschool Curriculum,* www.CathyDuffyReviews.com

True confession time: I am organizationally challenged! In certain seasons of life, my loving family, lesson plans, and literary pursuits get all out of whack. During a recent time of complete chaos, it was Marilyn Rockett to the rescue! Whether you are a little disorganized or totally cofused, Marilyn offers insight, inspiration, and ideas. You're gonna love this book!

—Christine Field

Author of *Homeschooling 101, Homeschooling the Challenging Child, Help for the Harried Homeschooler, Life Skills for Kids,* and others, www.HomeFieldAdvantage.org

Marilyn offers a fresh look at what comprises an orderly home and effectively how to achieve this goal. Rather than creating a program in which we feel enslaved, she promotes a lifestyle plan that enables us to view organization as our servant, not our taskmaster. For those who could use a "servant" around the house to help out, read on!

—Valerie Bendt

Author of *Reading Made Easy,* chosen as one of the *100 Top Picks for Homeschool Curriculum,* www.ValerieBendt.com

Marilyn Rockett has provided the perfect roadmap for your homeschooling journey. *Homeschooling at the Speed of Life* is a wonderful guide for newbies and veterans alike, a reminder to slow down and focus on God as we heed the call to teach our children at home, by putting one foot in front of the other down the twisting road of life.

—Debbie Williams

Organizing strategist, homeschooling mom, and author of *Organized Kidz: EZ Solutions for Clutter-Free Living,* www.organizedtimes.com

If you ever wanted an experienced homeschooler to come over to your house and help, consider this book. Inside, Marilyn Rockett explains how she earned her homeschool "PHD"—by "Praying for Help Daily." It shows! I have know Marilyn for years as a leader, speaker, writer, and homeschool mom. Reading this book has been a double delight for me. I got to savor the warmth, wit, and wisdom of an old friend while I anticipate how much she will bless homeschoolers. If you want to make wise use of the terribly short time that God has given you, buy this book!

—Scott Somerville
President of Lampstand Press, http://k-dad.net

I believe in homeschooling! I homeschooled for twenty-one years and continue to advocate for it now that my children are grown and on their own. In addition to the litany of duties every wife and mother faces, we are now expected to be curriculum experts, learning style gurus, teachers, field-trip guides, record keepers, and extracurricular coordinators. How can any mother possibly do all this?

Enter Marilyn Rockett. *Homeschooling at the Speed of Life* is the book I wish I had when I began my homeschooling journey. Marilyn brings hope to anyone who has ever struggled with the idea of having an orderly home and given up. She gives ideas that you can work into *your* schedule and way of doing things—while homeschooling.

Homeschooling at the Speed of Life is for *every* woman who is homeschooling—whether you are on the verge of quitting because you can't seem to get it all together or you want some solid ideas on how to make your home a vital center of ministry and hospitality. This book is based on Scripture and is full of hope and help.

—Zan Tyler
Author, speaker, and homeschool editor for Lifeway.com (www.lifeway.com/homeschool)

Reading *Homeschooling at the Speed of Life* is like having a loving older sister offer kind words, practical advice, and biblical guidance. This "older sister" is Marilyn Rockett—a veteran homeschool guru with both wisdom and a sense of humor. Chapter One alone is worth the price of the book! This book would make a great curriculum for training daughters, a lovely gift for a new mom, and an essential guide for your homsechooling friends. But first, do your family a favor and buy one for yourself. Newbies and veterans alike will be blessed by this important contribution to homeschool living.

—Maggie Hogan
www.BrightIdeasPress.com

Homeschooling at the Speed of Life is a restful sigh of RELIEF for homeschool moms everywhere. Once we bring our everyday life into some semblance of order, productivity increases and stress decreases. Marilyn Rockett is a gifted author with the ability to encourage and inspire. Home becomes a haven as Marilyn's techniques and advice are employed. My own eyes filled with tears as I related with her words. This book is highly recommended by *The Old Schoolhouse®* *Magazine.*

—Gena Suarez
Publisher of *The Old Schoolhouse®* *Magazine*, www.TheHomeschoolMagazine.com

HomeSchooling

at the speed of life

HomeSchooling
at the speed of life

Balancing Home, School, and Family in the Real World

B&H
PUBLISHING GROUP
Nashville, Tennessee

Marilyn Rockett

ISBN: 978-0-8054-4485-8

Published by B&H Publishing Group,
Nashville, Tennessee

Dewey Decimal Classification: 640
Subject Heading: HOME MANAGEMENT \ HOME ECONOMICS \
HOME SCHOOLING

Illustrations by Aruna Rangarajan

1 2 3 4 5 6 7 8 9 10   11 10 09 08 07

Dedication

I dedicate this book to my faithful husband, Chesley,
who has always believed in me more than I believed in myself,
who has moved me all over the country in the years of our
marriage, affording the opportunity for me to learn and grow more
than I thought possible, and who has worked hard to give our family
the privilege of a mom at home raising and teaching our sons.
I am forever grateful to you and love you more today than yesterday.

And to my four sons, Bill, Chris, Jonathan, and Jeremy,
who are the delights of my life.
You have made me understand, as close as I will this side of
heaven, what real love is. No higher degrees or accolades from any
source could take the place of the title I bear as your mom.
Thank you, to the three of you who are married, for choosing godly wives to
join our family (Carmen, Kimberly, and Mandy).
What a gracious God who gives me more than I deserve in all of you!
I praise Him for the blessing of your lives as part of mine.

Marilyn would like to hear from you.

If you have comments or ideas to share, the author would love to hear from you. Please send your own organization tips or stories of how this book helped you. Marilyn may use your contributions (when you include your permission and contact information) in her e-newsletter, "Timeminder Tips." Send to Marilyn@ MarilynRockett.com and visit her Web site at www.MarilynRockett.com. (She is unable to respond to requests for personal advice.)

Do you need a speaker for your group? Marilyn is available to speak on a variety of topics including organization, grandparents and homeschooling, and a unique mentoring seminar—Passing the Baton. You may e-mail her or visit the Web site for more information.

Go to www.lifeway.com/homeschool for more information on homeschooling.

Contents

Acknowledgments

Thank you for reading
these acknowledgments.

Many people skip the acknowledgments when they're eager to begin reading a book. They speculate that it isn't of interest to them—just thanks from the author to God and half the world for helping the author write the book. They want to get to the *meat* inside that applies to them.

Yet no author writes a book in a vacuum. Many people—family, friends, and some who are mere acquaintances—have had an influence on the author's life, affecting who that author has become and what he or she writes. When you read the acknowledgments, you get a small peek into the author's life, so it is often worth your while to take that moment to see what the author has to say.

This book has been in my heart for forty years. When I was a young woman, I prayed continually for a Titus 2 woman to come alongside me, but our family moved so frequently that it never was a blessing I could claim. When we began to homeschool, I cried even louder to the Lord for that godly mentor, but more often than not I was met with reactions of disdain or, at best, incomprehension from older women that I would want to do such a thing as keep my children at home. In an effort to aid me in bringing order to my home and homeschool, I designed *The Time Minder,* a home and school planner in a three-ring binder, and I published a few copies thinking friends could use them as well. I didn't realize at the time where those copies of a desperate mom's remedy would carry me.

I learned that I was in good company with other mothers who were struggling to make it all work as the homeschool movement grew. Writing articles, speaking to homeschool groups, and, after completing homeschooling, working as an editor and then managing editor for a national homeschool magazine gave me opportunity to share what I was learning with other homeschoolers as we traveled a new road of home-keeping while homeschooling. Moms were thirsty to hear anything that might give them help and hope for their eternal task. I continually said to the women in those groups, "Share what you are learning. Pass it on to someone else. Be an encouragement to another homeschool mom, and don't quit sharing when your children are grown and you have finished homeschooling."

Then one day not long ago it occurred to me—God was fashioning me into that Titus 2 woman that I had longed for in my young life. He wouldn't waste the years or the experience. He won't waste them with your life either. Share with someone else and keep on sharing.

God used my three-hole-punched forms in a three-ring binder to touch hearts and encourage souls that they were doing something important. It wasn't the sheets themselves, of course, but what the sheets represented—help to keep the balls in the air in the daily juggling act.

Hundreds of unnamed people (men and women) since that small beginning have blessed me with encouragement through the struggles and stories they have shared freely by e-mail and at homeschool conferences. I wish I could remember each of them by name, but I thank them here and hope I meet them in heaven where I will remember. They are among the most creative homeschoolers anywhere. Thanks most recently to Morgan, Laura, and Erin for sharing stories for this book.

Others that I can call by name and, more importantly, call my friends have been a blessing beyond measure to me. Mary Jo, Marti, Deb, Cathy D., Ruth, Debbie, Katie, Beverly, Maggie, Cathy J., Michele, Christine, Patt, and Stacy prayed for me, encouraged me, edited and read for me, helped with my Web site, made suggestions, and contributed stories for this book. Thank you, dear friends. You have made my life richer in your sacrifice of precious time to come to my aid.

When Zan Tyler, former homeschool resource and media consultant for B&H Publishing Group and current homeschool editor for Lifeway.com's Web network, www.lifeway.com/homeschool, called me to discuss this book project, I was elated. I always counted Zan as a dear friend from past homeschool days, and now I've been able to benefit directly from her many talents and abilities. Zan's encouragement, expertise, patience, and heart for homeschooling have been a blessing to me in this process. Thank you, Zan. I see why the Lord chose you for this job.

I am also delighted to write for such a fine publishing company as B&H Publishing Group. David Webb, executive editor, has been a delight to work with. David's talents are a boon to B&H. He understands homeschooling and homeschoolers, is superbly knowledgeable and efficient, and wants B&H products to be the best in the marketplace. He earns my high marks because he has displayed immense patience with my many e-mails with questions. Thank you, David.

Others at B&H that I've had the pleasure of working with on this project are Sheila Moss, outside editor; Kim Overcash, managing editor; and Stephanie Huffman, former homeschool marketing specialist. With her excellent input and editorial skills, Sheila has shown me why even an editor who writes needs a good editor. It is always a pleasure to work with an editor who displays such kindness in her corrections! Kim and Stephanie have reinforced the reasons that I'm glad to be writing for B&H—they have been efficient in their portions of the project while being considerate and helpful to me. I can speculate that they are representative of all the wonderful folks at B&H who work as a team to produce outstanding products. With such a team, homeschoolers will benefit immeasurably by having helpful and inspiring products that were not available in the early days of home education. I'm amazed and grateful and even a little jealous. (Perhaps I need to find some children to help homeschool. Oh, maybe that's what grandchildren are for!)

Thanks goes to my precious husband and my four sons, who are the reasons I have anything to say at all. The lessons they taught me in our family life are the reasons I could persevere.

The younger boys are probably happy that I waited to write this book until they were grown, especially since they were my shipping department when I published and sold *The Time Minder*. That twenty-five cents per package seemed like a good deal to them then! Thank you, precious sons, for the privilege of calling you my children.

I apologize to my patient husband for the occasional neglect that he endured while I wrote. This project came at a stressful time in his work, but he never complained. (Is there ever a convenient time to do something like write a book?) I'm glad Chesley knows how to cook and even likes it. On one occasion of late writing, I found him watching the food channel on TV and enjoying the program. He said he was looking for new ideas in case my project took longer than

I expected. Thank you, Chesley, for being my rock in difficult times. God has used you to make me a better wife and mother, able to share with others because of you.

Thank you, reader, for taking this small look into why this book is in your hands. I pray it is a blessing to you.

Getting Started

Make a trip to a large office supply store, and you will likely discover an overwhelming array of calendars, planners, date books, and organizers to choose from. The proliferation of these tools has made its way into homeschooling circles as well. Yes, organization has become a byword in our busy culture. Life moves swiftly, and most people are merely hanging on to accomplish all they need to accomplish and to keep up the pace. Books, seminars, and tools of all kinds are available to those of us who struggle to bring order out of chaotic living. Some businesses even offer in-home organization services. I know of one that charges fifty dollars per hour with a minimum of three hours. It's a desperate woman who allows a stranger to come into her home and open her closet doors!

With all this help available, why are you reading this book? With all these tools at your disposal, why haven't your efforts produced the results—the home—you hoped for? And why does getting organized seem so difficult?

My desire is that you find this book different from others you have read. I pray that you close the last page saying something like, "I can do this! I have hope again that things will *not* stay the way they are now. I *can* get the wash done and math taught at the same time. I *can* do what God has called me to do in keeping my home and educating my children." If your renewed hope is the result of my sharing many years of homemaking experience and involvement in homeschooling, I will rejoice with you. More important, you will reap an eternal outcome for you and your family.

Organized or Disorganized?

In all likelihood you have a preconceived mental image of your organizational self—basically organized but always looking for ways to improve (you actually enjoy reading books like this), struggling in some areas but getting along well in others, or a rather hopeless case on a continual quest for ways to climb out of the mire. By the way, I have never met a woman who thought she was so organized that she didn't need additional help; you can begin by forgetting any false notions of a supermom that you need to emulate.

What do you picture when you imagine yourself organized? In your dreams, are you always on time? Do you never lose your keys? Does your family get to church, or anywhere, with everyone wrinkle-free and wearing clean socks? Do you picture your family ready at any time to appear on the cover of a homeschooling magazine? Is your ideal mom a woman who breezes through the routine of life with a white glow surrounding her, moving from one task to another effortlessly? If so, wake up!

My purpose is not to fashion such a woman in you. Rest assured, she only lives in your dreams.

Yes, you may have legitimate reasons for why you aren't organized. Someone may not have trained you well. No one trained me.

You may have a basic lazy streak. Ouch! If you sincerely want to change, God may show you some rather unpleasant things about yourself. He did that for me.

You may have a latent rebellious spirit concerning your role in the home. Because of a perfectionistic mother who made you do all the chores she didn't like to do, you may be determined not to follow her example of keeping a "perfect" home.

You may be a right-brain-dominant person who can create almost anything but order.

You simply may be too busy. How many of us, after all, have *spare* time?

What Organization Is NOT

Becoming organized is difficult if you don't have a clear definition of what organization really is. You don't know where to set expectations if you haven't identified its distinctive. Having years and experience behind me, I realize there are some things that organization is *not*.

What words come to mind when you think of organization? *Scheduled? Meticulous? Rigid? Confining? Strict? Punctilious?* (I had to throw that last one in!)

You may not readily admit it, but many times you probably think organization is negative—we all do. When you operate from this point of view, even subconsciously, it's easy to give in to fear, dread, or guilt when you aren't fully organized; and you may abandon your well-intentioned efforts before you even get started.

May I challenge your thinking? Organization is none of the following things: perfectionism, neatness, cleaning (take a big sigh of relief and read on), or rearranging. It isn't a *Better Homes and Gardens* showplace that is a monument to your homemaking genius. A perfect home is not and should not be the goal. Rather, our calling is to a God-honoring home.

What Organization Is

As of this writing an estimated 6.5 billion people inhabit the world. Since God is quite resourceful and creative, we can be certain that no two of these people are exactly alike. However, our differences go beyond mere variations in physical characteristics. Even though each of us has different experiences, different ways of responding to a situation, different skills and abilities, different knowledge, and different interests and values, we have one very important similarity: each of us has the same number of hours in a day in which to balance who we are with the *dailiness* of life.

I dislike the popular term *time management*, and you won't find it again in this book. The realization that I can't manage time helped revolutionize my perception of organization. In fact, I can neither organize time, save time, nor spend time; and I certainly can't stop time! Managing time is God's responsibility—in our world and in our lives. Our only true option is to *use* time, and whether we use time in a positive or a negative way, its earthly constraints are gone forever.

Your challenge is to use time in a way that is effective for you and your family while you homeschool, keep your home functioning day to day, help your children become fully who they are, and become the person God created you to be.

With these thoughts in mind, I define *organization* in the following way:

> *Organization is making your life work for you*
> *by bringing the dailiness of life under control*
> *through yielding to the Holy Spirit*
> *concerning the wise use of your time.*

God asks us to yield to Him, allowing Him to order our lives in a way that will bring Him honor and glory. We certainly have a part to play in bringing to fruition this important end, and that is what this book is about.

Order Out of Chaos

My purpose is to encourage you and, in practical ways, help you move closer to the goal of keeping a God-honoring home. In the end, if all you have to show for your efforts is a beautiful home, an ordered schedule, and well-educated children without a heart for the Lord, you have not used your time wisely.

God has called you to this amazing, challenging, and difficult task of managing a home and educating the next generation of His children for His glory. He isn't surprised by your failures, nor is He especially impressed with your small victories. He knows that you have insecurities and feelings of inadequacy, and He delights that those imperfections drive you to trust Him more; *He* wants to be your adequacy rather than see you counting on your own accomplishments. In 2 Corinthians 12:9–10 He tells us that His grace is sufficient and that His power is perfected in our weakness. When we are weak, He is strong in our lives.

Managing a home and educating children will take you down corridors you never imagined you would go; some of them will be uncomfortable and inconvenient while others will be the most fulfilling and rewarding places you have ever been. God is in all those places—not just *with* you but *leading* you. He designed you and your unique family, and He will fulfill His purposes in your home as it brings Him honor.

This book isn't merely about the theory of home management. Conversely, it isn't *1001 Methods from Marilyn*. I won't ask you to implement *my* plan for *your* household. I will ask you to discover the plan that works for you and give you some direction to help determine that plan. I will ask you to roll up your sleeves and do some work as you proceed through these chapters. If you will do so, you will produce and enjoy positive change in your home.

I also offer you my prayers as you read and discern what the Lord would have you do to honor Him more fully. The Holy Spirit will guide you as you listen to Him. Whether you are just starting out as a homeschooling family or you're a veteran in need of a fresh start, I encourage you to offer up everything you do—from your most mundane household tasks to ministry to others—as a sacrifice of praise to Him. This is your calling, and He is able to complete the task in you.

Now, let's get started.

Chapter 1
Foundation for Organization
A Walk through the Word

Once upon a time (what seems like a very short time ago) in a land not really so far away, there was a very ordinary girl—just an ordinary Cinderella—who met her Prince Charming, married, had a houseful of little princes, and lived happily ever after.

But wait; in all the stories, the happily-ever-after part comes *before* the houseful of little princes and princesses and *before* the rust sets in on Prince Charming's armor. Time passes, and we never know if they truly lived happily ever after. All the parts between are conveniently left out. Isn't that what makes them fairy tales?

I grew up with the Cinderella Syndrome, dreaming of my Prince Charming, envisioning the happily-ever-after but not having a clue about the reality of life. Yet, unlike Cinderella, I wasn't prepared for the difficulties of managing a household and raising a family. No one trained me to care for a home and children. My family employed a maid six days a week. That may sound like heaven to you, but it handicapped me in adulthood, marriage, and motherhood. The first time I ironed a shirt with my mother-in-law present was one of those never-forgotten, embarrassing moments of my life. I didn't even know which end of the ironing board to use! She gently suggested that I try the other end of the board to make my task easier. When I made gravy for the first time (and in those days every Southern woman knew how to make gravy), I could stand a spoon upright in the bowl, and it would stay there; worse—I didn't know how to fix it!

Consequently, as a young wife, I vowed that my daughters would know how to do the necessary tasks to handle a household without feeling helpless and frustrated. God had such a sense of humor when He gave me four sons and not even one daughter! Undaunted, I set out to learn all I could—often the hard way—about caring for a home and family, and I began to teach my boys as I learned. After all, I reasoned, even men need to know a few practical things about the inner workings of a household in order to lead a family and to be equipped to help their wives in times of pregnancy or illness. Besides, I hoped to have daughters-in-law one day who would bless me because my sons knew how to do laundry, to keep a house reasonably clean, and to cook. They would appreciate it if their new husbands understood that clean shirts didn't magically appear in the closet and that the floor stayed clean because of someone's hard work. The princes would know how to take care of the castle.

There was one advantage in starting from scratch: I had no preconceived ideas about how to do most any chore. I simply looked for the best and fastest way to get it done. I found my own methods, and I wasn't afraid to experiment to discover the best one for me. Our home ran rather smoothly considering I was an amateur, until God brought homeschooling into my life.

> ## The challenge is not to manage time, but to manage ourselves.
>
> —Steven Covey, *hppt://quotations.about.com*

There were two things I said I would never do: teach school (my sister is the schoolteacher) and stay at home all day with children, doing "nothing." I boasted, based on my sixties, feminist-influenced background, that I could handle a family *and* employment outside the home at the same time.

However, God was working, with a smile no doubt, in my heart and life. He saved me. Then He saved my husband, and He gave us a son with an asthmatic condition from the age of six weeks, making it almost impossible for me to hold an outside job. As I stayed home and nursed a sick child, God showed me the calling that would honor and glorify Him. Of course, He had to accomplish those things before He brought homeschooling into my life. My heart was open and ready in 1981 when He did that.

By the time we began our homeschooling adventure, I had reasonably mastered the basics of keeping a home—at least on most days. But could I keep up with our usual busy schedule and add schooling as well? I quickly realized that, with this life-changing addition, I would need to fine-tune my organization habits. I wanted to avoid the pain and the consequences of disorganization, but I didn't realize at the time that I would need to work on some new skills and to reevaluate my understanding of organization within a homeschooling lifestyle.

Foundation from the Word

I fled to the Word to see if God had anything to say about organization, and I discovered, not surprisingly, that He offered wise counsel for a firm foundation. God has created us uniquely different, and we will each have our unique way to implement our plans, but the foundation of God's principles and commands remains the same for every Christian.

Why worry about organization? Why does it matter? Won't our lives work out just fine if we love the Lord, love our children, and do our best, even if things are chaotic at times? My exploration of the Word showed me that I was acting against God's plan when I thought I could ignore those important questions. I found six principles that laid a foundation that would hold my plans steady, even on my worst days.

Principle One: God's Design

We can't ignore God's design. He is a God of order—an elementary principle that we teach our very youngest children but that we forget to apply in our own lives. The first chapter of Genesis tells us that God created time as part of His creation, and He called that creation good. Time belongs to God to do with as He wills (Exodus 9:5). We don't always understand why God does the things He does when He does them, but we agree with the psalmist when he tells us in Psalm 31:15, "The course [plan] of my life is in Your power." Daniel 2:21 tells us that it is God who changes the times and the seasons.

> # If my private world is in order, it will be because I am convinced that the inner world of the spiritual must govern the outer world of activity.
>
> ## —Gordon MacDonald, *Ordering Your Private World*

Principle Two: God's Plans

Because God is a God of order, He plans. The Word gives us such an amazing picture of God's intricate plans—for His world and for us, His children. His plans aren't general, as though He created the world and then left it spinning on its own. No, He has very specific, detailed plans for His creation.

Isaiah 14:24 and 26 show us His involvement in our world: "The Lord of Hosts has sworn: As I have planned, so it will be; as I have purposed it, so it will happen. . . . This is the plan prepared for the whole earth, and this is the hand stretched out against all the nations." We see this sovereignty further in Psalm 33:10–11: "The Lord frustrates the counsel of the nations; He thwarts the plans of the peoples. The counsel of the Lord stands forever, the plans of His heart from generation to generation."

Yet God doesn't confine His planning to only global issues. He planned the tabernacle (Exodus 25—28) and the temple in which His people would worship Him and in which He would dwell. It is astounding that the Lord of the entire universe would want to be near His people and would plan, down to the smallest detail, to do so. First Chronicles 28:11–19 shows us the intricacy of God's plans. In part it says, "Then David gave his son Solomon the plans for the vestibule of the temple and its buildings, treasuries, upper rooms, inner rooms, and the room for the place of atonement. The plans contained everything he had in mind for the courts of the Lord's house, all the surrounding chambers, the treasuries of God's house, and the treasuries for what is dedicated. . . . David concluded, 'By the Lord's hand on me, He enabled me to understand everything in writing, all the details of the plan'" (vv. 11–12, 19).

This specific planning simply foreshadowed His greatest plan—our redemption—as He chose every part for our good and for His glory. Ephesians 1:11–12 tells us, "In Him we were also made His inheritance, predestined according to the purpose [plan] of the One who works out everything in agreement with the decision of His will, so that we who had already put our hope in the Messiah [Christ] might bring praise to His glory." God had the smallest details in mind in bringing us to Himself. Can you let that fully sink in? God plans precisely the thing that is most important—your redemption. How awe inspiring!

Principle Three: God's Image

God created us in His image (Genesis 1:27), and the desire for order and form that rises up in us is part of how He made us. We have His character, and we function best according to His plan. Ignoring God's plan produces confusion, frustration, and defeat. Warnings in Scripture, as in Proverbs 21:30, tell us that our plans must not go contrary to the Lord or they will fail: "No wisdom, no understanding, and no counsel will prevail against the Lord." When we fail to plan and we don't use our time wisely, our frustration rises from the chaos and confusion, but it also comes from the fact that we are disharmonious with the way God designed us.

Principle Four: God's Command

God tells us to plan. I would savor the luxury of doing what I want, when I want, and how I want, all the time. But that indulgence usually leads me into traps of my own making—disorder, lack of productivity, and a costly price for my unwise choices. However, Isaiah 32:8 reminds me that "a noble person plans noble things; he stands up for noble causes."

God gives instruction to His people to do things decently and in order because that reflects who He is. Chaos in the things we do, whether it's in our worship or our homes or our lives, does not please Him.

If we desire a wise heart before God, He tells us, in Ecclesiastes 8:5b–6a, that a wise heart knows the proper time and procedure for everything. My favorite Proverb relating to planning is Proverbs 14:22: "Don't those who plan evil go astray? But those who plan good find loyalty [love] and faithfulness." We have a wonderful God who understands we would rather not do what we need to do and gives us the encouragement to do it anyway!

A house is built by wisdom, and it is established by understanding; by knowledge the rooms are filled with every precious and beautiful treasure.

—*Proverbs 24:3–4*

Principle Five: God's Provision

God provides for us through plans—His and ours. Scripture is abundant with reminders that God encourages us to make plans and that His plans are for our good. We find a small sampling of those encouragements in the following verses:

May He give you what your heart desires and fulfill your whole purpose [plan]. (Psalm 20:4)

Teach us to number our days carefully so that we may develop wisdom in our hearts. (Psalm 90:12)

The plans of the diligent certainly lead to profit. (Proverbs 21:5)

"For I know the plans I have for you"—this is the LORD's declaration—
"plans for your welfare, not for disaster, to give you a future and a hope."
(Jeremiah 29:11)

*And my God will supply all your needs according to His riches in glory in
Christ Jesus.* (Philippians 4:19)

Often time seems like an enemy as the minutes squeeze your day tighter and
tighter and you see that you have more to do than you have time to complete. Do
you complain about not having enough time? Do you wish there were more hours
in a day? If you have toddlers, you may wish for *fewer* hours in your day because
bedtime seems much too far away for your exhausted body. As you witness your
children growing up right before your eyes, do you wish that you could stop time
before those precious moments slip away?

In those instances I have to remind myself that time is a gift from God. An
Irish proverb says, "Time is so precious that it is dealt out to us only in the smallest possible fractions—a tiny moment at a time."[1] Just as a beautiful, delicate
flower unfolds slowly, one petal at a time, God protects us within the layers of
His created time, unfolding each day lovingly and gently as He reveals, day by
day, His perfect plans for our lives. When we are aware and when we remind
ourselves that God is continually meeting our needs and urging us to make plans
that will benefit us and bring Him glory, we experience God's deep peace—the
antidote to chaos.

Dost thou love life? Then do not
squander time, for that is the stuff
life is made of.

—Benjamin Franklin, *http://quotations.about.com*

Principle Six: God's Lessons

God teaches us to trust Him in the midst of our plans. We often forget that He is the one in control and that we should hold our own plans very loosely in open hands, allowing Him to change those plans when needed. He asks us to trust Him when He cancels our plans to implement His.

God is never late; He is always on time. When I was pregnant with our third son, God gave me a vivid picture of how He is on time and how I can trust Him with my plans.

After numerous attempts and tears to acquire a beautiful, white wooden changing table that I thought I had to have, I finally gave up. When I tried to convince my husband that I really *needed* it, he was adamant that we couldn't purchase it at that time.

Then one day at a yard sale, I saw one that was very similar to the one I had coveted in the local furniture store. I couldn't believe it! God seemed to be meeting my desire and for less money—much less. When I inquired, I learned that the owner had sold the changing table to a man who planned to return and pick it up. That seemed impossible; surely God wasn't snatching away what He had allowed me to find.

I uncertainly gave my phone number to the owner, in case the man failed to return, but I had lost my faith that God would provide what I needed. Under conviction by the Holy Spirit, my heart was heavy until I surrendered to the Lord's plan, asking Him to make me willing to accept the loss of my treasure. I was willing to be willing, but I needed the Lord's help.

One week later when the phone rang, I was surprised to hear the woman from the yard sale on the other end of the line. She announced that the man had never returned for the changing table even though he had paid twenty dollars for it. She was moving that day and had left it on the street for me to pick up if I wanted it. The trash service would pick it up if I didn't come for it.

I was elated and humbled. You see, the Lord's plan wasn't to allow me to purchase an inexpensive changing table, as I thought. He wanted to *give* me a changing table. He also wanted me to trust Him when I couldn't see the end of my own plans. He had plans for my provision that were better than my plans. As Paul instructs in Philippians 4:19, "My God will supply all your needs according to His riches in glory in Christ Jesus."

Now we can return to my definition of *organization*:

Organization is making your life work for you
by bringing the dailiness of life under control
through yielding to the Holy Spirit
concerning the wise use of your time.

The foundation is in place: design (seeing our life work by God's plan because we are functioning according to His design for us); plan (bringing the dailiness of life under control); obedience (yielding to the Holy Spirit by allowing God to meet our needs and change our plans); wisdom (trusting God to teach us to determine the wisest use of our time).

Making those choices, as we yield to the Holy Spirit, is a challenge to our rebellious hearts. However, the foundation must be in place if we are to live a life that honors and glorifies the Lord even while we clean our closets and teach our children. Ephesians 5:15–16 reminds us that we must be careful how we live our lives (not as unwise, but as wise) as we make the most of the time God gives us.

When [God] gave us the limits of time and finiteness, at that moment He also built in the necessity of balance.

—Richard A. Swenson, MD, *Margin*

You will read the concept of balance often in these pages. If you love the Lord, you will want to be the same person inside that you appear to be on the outside. You want God to grow you and change you. He will supply all your needs as you plan to build on His firm foundation and do your part to obey Him.

I have designed this book to help you make real progress toward your goal of an orderly and God-honoring home. Use it as a workbook, answering the questions at the end of each chapter on the note page provided, or use a separate notebook to work through the exercises. Feel free to leave blank any questions and exercises that aren't beneficial to you, but I encourage you to make use of all parts that will direct you toward your goal.

Stop, Look, Think

Direction—Where Are You Going?

1. Do you see yourself as organized, unorganized, or somewhere in between? After reading "Getting Started" and this chapter, would you change the way you think about being organized? How?
2. Have your organization resolutions only led to failure in your efforts? Record your thoughts about your failures and your victories.
3. On a three-by-five card write the definition of *organization* from "Getting Started" and in this chapter and post it where you can see it often (your bathroom mirror, the refrigerator, a bulletin board, screen saver on your computer monitor, etc.)
4. Based on the definition of organization, are you using your time wisely to bring your dailiness under control? Make a list of the things you want to change.

Devotion—What Are You Thinking?

1. Look up the following Scriptures: Genesis 1:3–5; Job 24:1; Exodus 26:30; 1 Chronicles 28:11–19; 2 Chronicles 3—4; Ecclesiastes 8:5b–6a; Jeremiah 29:11; Ephesians 5:15–16, and review the six foundational principles in this chapter, looking up any other verses that come to mind.
2. Ask the Lord to show you any areas where your attitudes or actions are contrary to His design for you. With which of the six principles do you need to commit your heart to the Lord for His working (God's Design, God's Plans, God's Image, God's Command, God's Provision, God's Lessons)?

Notes

Chapter 2
Real-life Home Management
The Basics

Perhaps you've heard or read that homeschooling isn't just an education method; it's a lifestyle or a learning lifestyle. I heartily agree with the philosophy that promotes academics blended into life to meet the individual needs of your children and that admonishes you to gain your children's hearts while in pursuit of their excellent education. One size in education certainly doesn't fit all children.

However, that's not my focus in this book. While incorporating home teaching into a learning lifestyle rather than producing a classroom replica can certainly smooth the process, balancing household work and family needs with homeschooling is still a challenge. Some families have abandoned the homeschool effort simply because mothers have struggled with home-keeping while schooling their children. How sad to give up this rewarding and eternal endeavor because of a pile of laundry or a sink full of dirty dishes!

Everyone faces at least two problems: First, how do we balance who we are—our particular personality challenges—with doing a good job managing our homes? The distance from our heads to our hearts is the longest eighteen inches in the world; and even when we know what to do, we struggle to do it. Second, how do we bring the dailiness of life under control? As life speeds by, we often feel as though we are contestants on a television game show, with the clock ticking a warning that time is almost up and we'll lose the prize if we don't finish in time.

> Failure is simply the opportunity to begin again, this time more intelligently.
>
> —Henry Ford, *http://quoteworld.org*

Even if you think there is no hope for you because you're so disorganized, you *can* have an orderly home. I admit that it's easier for some personalities than for others; some thrive on order and will go to great lengths to achieve it. Nevertheless, no matter how deep you've sunk into disorganization, you can make progress toward a home that honors the Lord. The nagging guilt that hangs over your head when you ignore a necessary task is worse than actually getting that necessity done. Obedience to the Lord calls you to determine what you need to change and to follow through with that change. It doesn't matter what your circumstances are or how many children you have; there are families with two children who struggle with chaos, and families with ten children who live in peace and order.

I've decided that time is like closets. No matter how much time or how many closets you have, you fill them up! You have the choice of filling both with constructive, helpful things or with wasteful, useless things. While it's human nature to drift to the easy task, the enjoyable activity, or the urgent rather than the necessary, you can change the way you respond to filling your time.

People and Things

Would you keep the following important principle in mind as you read farther?

People are more important than things,
but things out of control hinder our relationships with people.

We're all aware of the dangers of putting things above people and that relationships *are* profoundly important to our lives. Otherwise we wouldn't bother to make the sacrifices we do in order to homeschool. However, it's surprisingly easy to overcompensate by placing people so high above things that we neglect things and ultimately end up hurting people as well. People *are* more important than things, but you can't omit the second part of the principle and still maintain balance.

> Every wise woman builds her house,
> but a foolish one tears it down with
> her own hands.
>
> —*Proverbs 14:1*

Think for a moment about the way your home currently functions. Are you or your family members constantly losing things and continually growling at an offender about keeping up with possessions? Are you late most of the time because you are scurrying to complete last-minute tasks before you walk out the door? Do you nag your children to do their chores but fail to follow up to see that they complete them? Does your spouse have a different standard of orderliness from yours? Do you want to invite guests to your home but do so infrequently because your cluttered home is embarrassing? Does having guests for dinner require a major cleaning day before they arrive? Or forget dinner—simply dessert and coffee would be nice! Do you close the doors to the bedrooms and pray that no one goes there? These are just a few of the ways that disorder affects our relationships with family, friends, and acquaintances and impedes us from the pure joys of living.

If your heart desires a home of peace, order, and welcome, where do you start? Let's begin with priorities and look at ten basics for real-life home management.

Ordinary people think merely
of spending time. Great people
think of using it.

—Author Unknown, *http://quotations.about.com*

Establish Priorities

Crisis and established habits have possibly been the foundation for most of your choices because it's easier to respond by default than by design. However, with priorities firmly established, you can fill your time with the best choices while maintaining control and a sense of direction.

Your priorities will be different from your best friend's priorities. You must learn to sift out the things that don't fit and to live your life based on *your* priorities rather than on those of others.

Living by your priorities means making some difficult choices. A conscious choice of something that is beneficial to you and your family is better than a choice by default. Sometimes it's even effective to choose what you're *not* going to do by eliminating something in your life or substituting a different activity. If you attempt to participate in every activity available for every child in the family, you'll be running so fast that your home will fall apart.

Your family priorities should dictate your school and outside activities rather than the reverse. Be willing to look critically at the things that consume your time: too much computer time, too little thought about household necessities, too many activities, too many days away from home, and so on.

If your home is out of balance, your enjoyment of the important things will be limited, and your home will not reflect the Lord. The cultivation of both a family and a personal mission statement can help remedy this problem. This book's accompanying CD includes a sample family mission statement and a blank form for your use.

> # When you discover your mission, you will feel its demand. It will fill you with enthusiasm and a burning desire to get to work on it.
>
> —W. Clement Stone, *www.wisdomquotes.com*

A good beginning is to sit down with family members who are old enough to contribute to the discussion and decide what is most important to the family. All adults and older children can form personal mission statements as well. Fill in the blanks for these statements: Our family purpose is _____. (My purpose is ____.) Does _____ [a specific activity] fit our (my) purpose? List as many activities as needed. Of course, priorities or purposes may change with different seasons of your life.

This exercise will produce a list of central priorities that must be in place—education has to take place in some fashion, and you must do basic home chores and maintenance. Work and worship would be central to your priorities as well. Beyond those points, you can add to your list based on an agreed-upon purpose or mission for the year and upon your family size, children's ages, and available time. Actually recording your priorities on paper helps crystallize the purpose in everyone's thinking; it's easier to see which things are causing overload when you realistically see what is taking your time. The Family and Personal Mission

Statement Form on the CD is flexible and is simply an example. If this method doesn't seem to fit your family and personal need, use another way that works for you to record your priorities. Just keep it simple and add more items as they come to mind. It is usually ineffective to make a linear list since we have equally important priorities in various areas of our lives. For example, a numbered list of priorities (1, 2, 3, and so forth) won't serve you as well as a list or diagram that designates priorities in areas of your life. Make the mission statement your tool rather than your master.

Set Goals and Plan Ahead

Priorities give you a vision and direction; goals become the legs to your priorities. They are the means by which you live and walk out your priorities as they hold you accountable for the things you say you plan to do. In fact, I'm convinced that goals are directly linked to motivation. Goals help you see the ultimate picture of what you want your home, school, and life to be like; and they help move you in that direction.

Lord, help me to set aside my shortsighted goals and desires and honestly seek Your will. Train my heart for contentment and guard it from the temptations of busy living.

—Stacy McDonald, *Raising Maidens of Virtue*

Why do some people seldom reach their goals? I've observed that it is because people don't know how to set goals properly. For success, goals must be simple, specific, measurable, and attainable. State goals in positive rather than negative terms. "I won't let the laundry pile up" is not a goal. "I will keep the laundry current and in the drawers/closets immediately after it's clean each week" is a positive goal. "I will wash one load of laundry per day, Monday through Friday, will fold the load before lunch, and will have the children put the clean clothes away after lunch" is a plan to reach that goal.

A goal isn't a desire; it is something you have the ability to accomplish. You cannot set a goal for someone else because other people's behavior is beyond your control. You cannot set a goal for your husband to put his socks into the laundry hamper; however, you can set a family goal and plan for all members to put their dirty clothes into the hamper immediately after undressing. That goal is simple, specific (a certain thing for someone to do), measurable (you can tell when the clothes are on the floor), and attainable (yes, in spite of your doubt).

People also fail to meet their goals when they overplan and try to accomplish too many things at once. Work on the things that bother you most or the things that are out of control before you tackle other problems. Begin where you are, but do begin. When you prioritize a problem and set a goal for changing it, you put the problem on track for a remedy. Your feeling of accomplishment when you see progress motivates you to solve other problems.

As I have observed homemakers, I see an important difference between the woman who accomplishes more and balances her many responsibilities and the one who does not. The resourceful woman foresees potential problems before they occur—like adding toilet paper to the grocery list when someone opens the last package rather than when the last roll is on the holder—and takes action to prevent those problems. She makes one trip to the grocery store rather than multiple trips for forgotten items. She addresses birthday cards ahead of time and shops early for gifts to prevent a last-minute run to the store for a special occasion. At night she puts out clothes for toddlers for the following morning, and she forestalls grouchy young children when dinnertime approaches by giving them a light snack in the afternoon. Some of these kinds of problems may be a starting place for your goal setting.

The method you use to record your goals isn't as important as actually writing them down in some form. You'll find sample goal sheets on the accompanying CD, but if these forms don't work for you, create some that do. The important point is to start with the areas that overwhelm you. Work on only two or three goals at one time. Post a goal sheet where you'll see it often and check yourself periodically. If you don't see progress, ask why. Are you ignoring your plan? Are you too ambitious with the number of goals you try to accomplish at once?

Do you need to modify your plan to solve the problem? Change the plan if it isn't helping you reach your goal, but don't give up. Continue to set goals and make plans to achieve them.

Keep It Simple Sweetie (KISS)

The old KISS method is always best. Don't be a slave to any system. Experiment with new ways to do things, but if you are spending more time writing, filing, sorting, and planning than you are in doing the things you need to do, your system needs to be amended. Planners and organizers are helpful tools, but don't tie yourself to a method that seems too complicated for you. Those who like less structure may use a simple calendar, and those who like planners may do better with a more structured method. This is the key question to ask: "Is what I'm using working?"

> # Organizing is what you do before you do something, so that when you do it, it is not all mixed up.
>
> —A. A. Milne, *http://quotationspage.com*

Since too many choices produce more problems, simplify your options and avoid overplanning. If you are overwhelmed, cut back now and add goals and activities later as you are able.

Organization "experts" often suggest timing your chores so you know what you can fit into a morning or an afternoon. However, my household never ran on a minute-by-minute clock. Invariably a toddler threw up or a toilet stopped up, demolishing any well-timed chore. However, I did find one benefit from timing a chore that I didn't like. I happily discovered that wiping out the refrigerator just before it was time to restock took only about ten minutes. The dreaded chore felt like it took much longer; but when I realized the short time it actually took, I was more inclined to get it done when I had ten minutes. If you procrastinate when you face unpleasant tasks, time them and resolve to take advantage of short windows of opportunity to accomplish those small jobs. Conversely, resolve to spend ten or fifteen minutes doing a job you can't seem to accomplish and then stop in the allotted time. If you aren't finished, you are further along than you were before those minutes, and you can return to finish the task at your next available opportunity. Remember: This principle applies to small jobs that normally take a short time to complete.

Keeping it simple means establishing a *simple*, basic routine based on a predictable sequence rather than a schedule of things to do at a certain time. A desperate mother once shared with me that she didn't know if she could ever be *that* organized, but I encouraged her not to ignore this easy concept. A routine for the basics is the single most helpful thing you can do to restore order to your home. A simple, skeleton routine maintained regularly gives you freedom and flexibility to enjoy other activities. (See the Master Household Routine sheet on the CD.) It also gives you specific, uninterrupted school time while still keeping your home in order. It isn't as hard as you may think, and it's much easier than a painful daylong marathon of housecleaning and lost time from productive school activities.

There is an occasion for everything,
and a time for every activity
under heaven.

—Ecclesiastes 3:1

If you haven't established a simple household routine, walk through your house room by room with a new view and with paper and clipboard or a notebook. See the Home Works Planner on the CD to guide you, if necessary. Divide your paper into quarters—a line down the middle of the page horizontally and another vertically. Label each quarter as follows: Daily, Weekly, Monthly, Annually (or Seasonally). Now divide each quarter into two columns and label one Essential and one Necessary. The distinction between the two categories is that items you absolutely must do or your home won't function are Essential; items that you need to do eventually but you can shift or delay are Necessary. As you enter a room, carefully look around. Write down everything needed in that room on a daily, weekly, monthly, or annual basis, evaluating whether each chore is essential or necessary and putting it under the appropriate column in the proper quadrant. For example, in the kitchen you might list *sweep the floor* and *wash the dishes* under Daily and Essential (you eventually run out of dishes), but you might put *clean the oven* under Monthly and Necessary. In a bedroom you would likely record *make the bed* under Daily and Essential and *vacuum* and *change the sheets* under Weekly and Essential. Dusting is a different issue; some consider it essential while others have decided that dust is a protective covering for their furniture! Remember, this is *your* list of things that you consider essential and those that might not be as important all the time.

Use this sheet to evaluate your household priorities; accomplish Essentials first. This sheet also reveals the areas in which you need to gain control. It reminds you of essential things that you are neglecting. It serves as a guide for goal setting. We will look at other uses for this sheet later in this chapter and in chapter 4.

Don't do things a certain way only because your mother did them that way. If she stayed home and didn't homeschool her children, for example, she had more time to keep her home. My mother kept all cleaning supplies in her pantry in our one-story home and took what she needed from there. However, it was impractical for me to follow that method in our two-story homes. I kept duplicate cleaning supplies stored in various rooms for quick access.

We must use time as a tool,
not as a crutch.

—John F. Kennedy, *http://quotationspage.com*

Look for shortcuts: use a basket or bucket to transport household tools with you as you and your children work; wear an apron with large pockets to tuck in those little items that you need to put someplace else; make a master grocery list so you don't waste time rewriting your normal purchases; save steps and time in every way you can.

When my sons studied the American pioneer era, I often wondered how those hardy frontier women accomplished so much with so few resources. I was a little ashamed by how I struggled to manage my household despite the many supposed time-saving conveniences I had at my disposal. One day, in a flash of realization, I clearly saw the answer to that puzzle—a pioneer woman didn't own an automobile! Her focus was her home, and her choices were simple. I realized that modern time-savers don't always make my life simpler if I don't use that "saved time" wisely to care for my home and family.

Write Things Down

Lists won't do your work for you; I wish they would. However, they will keep you on track and aid your memory as the day's urgencies swirl around you. But what kind of list is most effective? Different methods work best for different people. I felt boxed in by lists of things to do on a calendar and on other forms, such as a meal plan sheet. Just when I planned a day to complete errands and I recorded my list on a certain day, my toddler developed an infection or my ten-year-old required stitches in the emergency room. A running to-do list served me better than a calendar for all my to-do's.

You can create your own Running To-Do List in a small notebook. Any type is fine—fancy planner or plain notebook. Draw a line down the center of a page, front and back, producing four columns. Label the columns Errands, To-Do, Projects, and Nonemergency Tasks (more about that column in chapter 7). When you think of anything you need to do, record it on your list under the appropriate column. Don't worry about putting the list in a particular order. A trip to the dry cleaners or the library goes in the Errands column. Making phone calls to inquire about a field trip or a doctor's appointment go on the To-Do list, and sewing a costume for the homeschool co-op play goes under Projects.

If you tend to start projects and not finish them, write down all the details rather than a broad description of the task. For example, if you need to sew a costume, you would write *buy pattern and fabric* under the Errands column. Then you can record *cut out costume, sew, fit costume on Johnny,* and *make adjustments* in the Projects column. You can see the details you have to complete and check off each step as you do it. If you shiver at the thought of a list tucked away in a plan book, post your reminder on a bulletin board or in a prominent place, but use wisdom and don't let these postings grow to an unmanageable volume.

> # He who every morning plans the transactions of the day, and follows out the plan, carries on a thread which will guide him through the labyrinth of the most busy life.
>
> —Hugh Blair (1718–1800), *Sermons*

Write your lists in pencil. An eraser is wonderful! When you are ready to make a trip for your errands, number the ones you are doing that day in the order of the stops you'll make. This method keeps you from arriving home only to discover that you forgot one of your errands.

Check off or mark through completed items and keep the list going. Once you have filled your paper and completed your tasks, start another sheet. You may have to transfer a few remaining items to a new list, and this list won't look pretty; but life is rather messy, isn't it?

Keep one central calendar or planner rather than papers and notes scattered about. Those who write notes on scraps of paper are the ones who usually are most prone to losing them. Some people find that they function better with the combination of a calendar/planner they can transport in a purse at all times and a large family calendar hung at home where all can see it and record family activities. However, some mothers prefer just one calendar/planner so they have only one place to keep track of their life. Use what works for you. Children's chore charts can be an extension of your planner and to-do list. We'll discuss this further in chapter 4, "Teaching Children Life Skills." The important factor is to keep track of what you have to do by putting it in writing.

Begin Small

A distraught mother at a homeschool convention shared that even though it had been more than a year since her family moved, she was still facing piles of boxes to unpack. She had lost sleep thinking of the monumental task of unpacking them all, and the family was functioning with the bare necessities. Why wasn't she making progress in emptying the mountain that faced her? As we talked, I discovered that she couldn't get past seeing the entire pile of boxes, and she quit before she began because of her dread of the task.

Nothing can be done except little by little.

—Charles Baudelaire, *Little Things*

If you face a mountain of any kind, you must begin one step at a time. This mother needed to choose one box and start. Her plan could be to unpack one box per day until she finished the last box. Unpacking one box is doable and would lead her to the end of her task.

Begin where you are and first face the things that trouble you the most. Where to start, though, is usually less important than just starting. Use your Home Works Planner as explained earlier in this chapter to help you decide where to start. What Essentials listed there are tasks that need improvement right away? What do you struggle with most in your day-to-day effort to keep your home organized? What could you do immediately to help the situation? What could you do over a longer term to solve the problem?

For example, does your laundry pile high, and do you never catch up? (Yes, we all have rewashed clothes that sat so long in the basket or dryer that we had to do them again!) If you currently wash all your laundry once a week, try washing one load each day or one load three days a week instead—whites one day, coloreds one day, sheets/towels one day, and so forth. Wash and dry the load, immediately remove it from the dryer, fold or have your children fold, and put away everything before bedtime. You'll not only complete the wash, but your example will also teach your children to complete a job.

As you begin any task, apply these principles:

- Avoid all-or-nothing thinking; do something even if you can't do everything. When you don't know what to do, choose the thing that will produce peace in your mind.
- Forget thinking that you can get it all done at any one moment in time. There is always something else to do in a home, so relax and take care of what is before you.
- Enlist help from your family. See chapter 4 on "Teaching Children Life Skills" and set your family to working effectively.

Deal with Clutter

Ah, clutter! It earns its own chapter since it's the biggest time-binder that we face. We don't like to talk about it, and it frustrates us in multiple areas of our lives. When a friend and I began to homeschool, we commiserated by asking each other where to begin. Her humorous statement touched a vital truth: "I don't know where to start, but I think we should clean our closets!"

Clutter may be causing more difficulty in your life than you realize. It can affect not only the aesthetics but also the emotional, spiritual, and physical aspects of your life. The truth is that life is messy in all kinds of ways, and we have to face it eventually. Read on to chapter 3 for help with clutter.

Don't Compare

You and your family are a work in process by the Lord. Superwoman, superdad, and superchild don't exist in real life. When you read a book, hear a seminar speaker, or observe an admired friend, it can be tempting to feel as though you've failed if you aren't emulating that example. However, we each have struggles and weaknesses, and we each have strengths and something helpful to share with someone else. Learning from others is positive; comparing yourself to others is detrimental.

If you are discouraged, try to uncover the causes. Are you getting enough sleep? Are you taking care of your health? Are you doing too much and staying too busy? Are you a perfectionist who gives up because you can't do it all or do it best? Are you putting off the things you don't like to do? Are you looking at the negative in your situation rather than trusting that the Lord is in control? Are you spending time with the Lord, or has the urgent crowded out the important in your busyness?

> Fixing your gaze on someone else's path only pulls you off your own course. The discouragement you receive will most likely slow your progress.
>
> —Debbie Strayer, *Gaining Confidence to Teach*

Where are your expectations? Are you willing to decrease your expectations to obtain balance in your life and home? Maybe you need to increase your expectations if you have become lazy. You don't gain the confidence to teach your children and manage your home from your super abilities. That comes from a heart bowed before the Lord and dependance on Him as your source of strength. His calling for you is the only proper comparison to make in your life.

Be Flexible and Trust God

I wish planning meant nothing would go wrong, but we all know from experience that isn't true. Although you need structure, too rigid a system can create a different set of problems. You usually can't box life in the way you want to.

Distractions happen; expect them! There are times when you must simply stop and give attention to a problem before you can resume what you were trying to accomplish. You can't wait to discipline a toddler when that discipline is required now, and you can't ignore your children because of your well-planned schedule.

Life seldom goes as smoothly as we would like it to, but you can rest in the knowledge that because God wants you to have a successful family and an orderly home even more than you want them, He will guide you. You deal with a home full of people every day, unlike those who send their children away to school. You must flex to accommodate all the activity, changes, and disruptions; but it's easier to bend when you have a plan that returns you to your course.

> We shouldn't look at homeschooling as a recipe where you put in the perfect ingredients in just the right order and out comes a perfect product, as promised.
>
> —Debbie Strayer, *Gaining Confidence to Teach*

It's tempting to make school supreme during your day. Oh, I'm not saying that you shouldn't teach your children with excellence and spend ample time doing it. However, they are learning far more by living life in your home than the average child who goes away daily to a school setting. Your children are learning how to live, learn, and have relationships that will aid them all their lives. Keep your simple, basic routine as closely as possible; but flex when you have to for legitimate reasons. See chapter 7 to learn about a Ketchup Day to regroup. Your family, your children, and the things that come into your life aren't surprises to God. Praising the Lord for the messiness of life and the people who make those messes is much easier when you have a workable plan.

*Sloooow Down and Say **No***

There is no cure for overcommitment short of amputation of unnecessary activities. Most of us seem to believe that we can fit more and more into our lives without any consequence. We don't say no when we should, yet we wonder why we have difficulty keeping up the pace. We act as if there's a Scripture that says, "Busyness is next to godliness," but we haven't found the reference.

> One half the troubles of this life can be traced to saying yes too quick, and not saying no soon enough.
>
> —Josh Billings, *Little Things*

Others at church, in homeschool organizations, and in the community bring pressure on moms at home when they falsely conclude that she is available to do the jobs that no one else "has time" to do. In the meantime moms try to be all things to all people and hate to say no when called upon.

I'm not advising you to abandon all outside activities. Many of the lessons, classes, and activities the Lord provides can help you and your children achieve worthy goals. However, because a project is good in itself doesn't mean it's right for you and your family at a particular time; you must align your choices with your priorities. Use your gifts in your local church and participate where you are able. However, there are seasons in your life when some things are more appropriate and beneficial than others. Raising and teaching your children is the most important, long-reaching mission you'll accomplish with your life; and God has called you to that task.

Mom, are you prayerfully considering each opportunity that presents itself? Are you able to say, "I'll get back to you," when you are asked to fill a position or do a job? The list of family and personal priorities mentioned earlier is most useful for this area of your life. Evaluate whether the activity under consideration fits your priorities. How important is it to choose this particular thing? If you choose it, will you be able to do it with excellence and still keep balance in your home?

If you struggle with saying no when you know you should, allow your husband, or a trusted mentor if you are a single mom, to help you say no. Develop the habit of always responding with "I need to talk it over with my husband (mentor)" even when you think you should do what is asked of you. If you are pressured with a response such as, "Oh, we need you so much. No one else will (can) do the job," then that is increased reason to think it over. It's entirely possible that the Lord doesn't want the job done if He doesn't raise up the appropriate person to accomplish it. Why don't you practice saying *no* right now? It's easier than you think when you know that's what you can or should do!

> # The future is something which everyone reaches at the rate of sixty minutes an hour, whatever he does, whoever he is.
>
> —C. S. Lewis, *www.wisdomquotes.com*

Take Time for the Lord and for Rest

How does a mother find time for the Lord and time to refresh when she is busy serving those around her? There is only one way: she has to plan the time. It never just happens. Mothers aren't robotic machines that are still working twenty hours later without a break. Mothers need rest and refreshment in order to continue to serve their families. Don't be a martyr! Acknowledge that you need some personal time.

You must be aware of your personality and needs. Could you use a break for a few minutes each day? Do you need an hour in your bedroom talking to Jesus? A weekly time away for a few hours? An occasional weekend away? That's where husbands, grandparents, mentors, or friends can help. An understanding husband is a blessing, but don't wait for him to see the pressures you face. Without complaining, talk to him about ways he can help you. If he still doesn't respond to your need, plan times when a relative or trustworthy friend can help you. See chapter 7 for how to have a refreshing EDIT Day.

Seek any way possible to spend time with the Lord reading His Word. It doesn't have to be the traditional morning quiet time, which is often difficult for a mother of young children to accomplish. You may take a few minutes while the baby naps or while Dad bathes the children before bedtime. If you aren't exhausted, the best time may be a few minutes just before bedtime. One friend of mine keeps a Bible in her van, at her bedside, in the bathroom, and at other strategic places so she can read at each opportunity. As she said, "That way I can get a Word in edgewise!" Another mom with nine children has a willing husband who prepares breakfast with the older children while she has her quiet time in the morning. She joins the family at breakfast, refreshed and ready to meet the day. Remember that the Lord is your true strength and that your life is in Him. That time takes precedence over chores you think you must finish. If you are too busy to meditate on Scripture and to pray, you are out of balance.

> ## The One who is in you is greater than the one who is in the world.
>
> —*1 John 4:4b*

A Mother's Job Description

Daniel Webster said, "He that has a 'spirit of detail' will do better in life than many who figured beyond him in the university. Such an one is minute and particular. He adjusts trifles; and these trifles compose most of the business and happiness of life. Great events happen seldom, and affect few; trifles happen every moment to everybody; and though one occurrence of them adds little to the happiness or misery of life, yet the sum total of their continual repetition is of the highest consequence."[1]

That describes a mother's job perfectly! Aren't you always adjusting trifles? And the results of using your days wisely dealing with those trifles are of the highest consequence, affecting the lives of your children and those around you. Real life brings pressure for the difficult job of managing a home while home educating, and you must continually adjust and start again.

Persevere

Change, when needed, is difficult, isn't it? Life *is* daily; learn from your mistakes and move forward toward your goal. Don't you want to teach your children that too? If you haven't planned well, evaluate how you have failed and plan to do better. God is the one who is able, and His grace is boundless.

> Therefore, my dear [sisters], be steadfast, immovable, always excelling in the Lord's work, knowing that your labor in the Lord is not in vain.
>
> —*1 Corinthians 15:58*

In *Keep a Quiet Heart*, Elisabeth Elliot wrote: "God is not all we would ask for (*if* we were honest), but it is precisely when we do not have what we would ask for, and *only then*, that we can clearly perceive His all-sufficiency. It is when the sea is moonless that the Lord has become my light."[2]

Being a wife and mother, keeping a God-honoring home, and homeschooling your children will teach you to trust solely in the Lord more than any book or seminar. When you commit to persevere, He will honor that commitment and lift you up to fulfill your mission.

Stop, Look, Think

Direction—Where Are You Going?

1. Make a list of skills with which you struggle. What can you do to improve those areas?

2. Don't put it off any longer; make a family and personal mission statement and decide on your priorities right away. See the sample sheet on the CD, but remember it is only a guide to get you started. You should change, refine, expand, and adjust it to *your* family and *your* season of life.

3. Use the Home Works Planner on the CD or some other method to determine your home-keeping needs, and establish a simple household routine of essentials for your home, including school time. If you struggle with keeping a simple routine, put it in writing and post it for you and the family to refer to often.

4. From the above evaluation, determine what goals and plans you need to implement in your areas of struggle. Record them on one of the goal sheets included on the CD or use your own method. Check after one week, two weeks, and a month to see if your plan is moving you toward improvement. If not, find out why and make the necessary changes.

5. Is the method you use now for keeping up with your responsibilities working well? If not, how can you change it? The rare mother can manage her home well without writing anything down, but you may need to record more things than you are currently doing. Try something new if you are struggling.

Devotion—What Are You Thinking?

1. Ask the Lord to show you where you may need to change your expectations for your home, either lowering them or raising them as

necessary. Praise Him for being your strength to adjust to those new expectations. Read Psalm 29:11 and 2 Peter 1:3, and thank God for giving you all that you need to do your job.

2. Do you struggle with saying no when you should? Ask the Lord to help you sort out what you should do, when you should say no, and how to eliminate the excess from your life so that you honor Him.

3. Has your busyness swallowed up your time with the Lord? Read the following verses and mediate on them: 1 Chronicles 16:10–11; Psalm 73:25–26; 105:3–4; 138:2–3; Matthew 11:28–29; and Romans 12:1–3. Determine when you can be reasonably consistent in spending time with the Lord. Ask for help from your family to keep this time faithfully.

Notes

Chapter 3

Clutter, Clutter Everywhere and Not a Spot to Think

I have good news and bad news. The bad news is that talking about clutter is a little like talking to the IRS or to your doctor when he calls with test results. Or maybe like talking to your spouse when you made an error in the checkbook. Worse, it may be like talking to your in-laws about why you are homeschooling!

But you've come this far; keep reading. I'll save the good news for a bit later. For now, please recall the foundational principle that I mentioned in the last chapter:

People are more important than things,
but things out of control hinder our relationships with people.

We can all agree that people are more important than things, but dealing with clutter and things in your life helps you balance this principle.

Things are only useful when they don't hinder relationships with people and when they help you enjoy and serve the people around you. However, we humans have a problem: we have a magnetic attraction to *stuff*. Utopian-sounding gadgets, gimmicks, and gizmos, like the Roco Dooz It All, find their way into our homes, and before we know it, possessions possess *us*.

I like button-pushing conveniences as much as any modern mom, and my husband often reminds me that I'm blessed because I don't have to beat our clothes on a rock beside a river to clean them; however, most of us have more possessions than we truly use. If not, why would yard sales be so popular! Just check the bookstore shelves to see how many books there are on the topic of clutter. We live in a society that promotes accumulation—of things and of activities—as a way of life; but if our home is out of balance, having more can be a curse rather than a blessing.

Balance

Do you love your home right now? Is it a joy to live there? If not, somewhere between *Better Homes and Gardens* and the local junkyard, there's a place for you. Working for balance in your home concerning your things will bring order more quickly than any other aspect of your quest. Clutter is the largest reason you and your family can't clean quickly or well. Clutter slows you down and drains energy and joy from your life.

I know it's a struggle. Even when you make a concentrated effort to keep the clutter cleaned out, it still manages to stick its insidious nose in the door. The dailiness of life challenges you—all of us—to deal continually with stuff.

Logically you know it makes sense to clear away what you *don't* use in order to have room for what you *do* use. Even a large family doesn't need a lot of stuff. Yet we're emotional about our stuff. Once, when my family moved across country and rented a much smaller house, we put many things in storage. The move was to be somewhat temporary, but two-and-a-half years later, we were still there. The realization that we had moved those stored things cross-country, hadn't seen most of them since then, and hadn't even missed them was a sobering thought. Did we really need most things that had been stored for two-and-a-half years? It was time to clean out the clutter!

For where your treasure is, there your heart will be also.

—Matthew 6:21

Clutter Quiz

Are you brave enough to take a clutter quiz? How would you answer these questions?

1. Do you feel you must apologize for the mess or give an explanation when others come to your house, especially drop-in company?
2. Do you frequently lose things?
3. Do you find things that you forgot you had?
4. If you had to sell your home today, would you be able to show it to prospective buyers within a twenty-four-hour notice without embarrassment?
5. Do you have to search for regularly used items?
6. Are your closets so full that you constantly shuffle things to get to your needed items?
7. Do you have a multisize wardrobe for your always-changing body?
8. Have your collections taken possession of your home?
9. Do you have boxes in the attic or basement that only God knows for sure what they contain?
10. Do you attend yard sales regularly and come home with bargains you couldn't resist?
11. Do you have boxes of hobby, craft, or fabric projects that you will *someday* finish?
12. Do you have large or small broken objects that you or your spouse plan to repair and that have been broken longer than six months?
13. Do you have gifts that you dislike from relatives or friends, but you can't bring yourself to dispose of them?
14. Do you have one room or closet in your home that you have dubbed the "junk room"?

15. Have you decided to buy another file cabinet because you have filled all you have?

16. Are your kitchen cabinets full, but you use only 50 percent of what's there?

17. Does it take you and your children longer than forty-five minutes to an hour each day to clean and straighten your home? (A family can usually clean the home in two to three hours when once-a-week cleaning occurs.) This routine excludes such larger annual jobs as cleaning out the garage or washing windows. Yes, homeschoolers can find time to clean windows! Think what fun your kids can have wearing old clothes and washing windows in the summer—Tom Sawyer style. Moms of toddlers, you are exempt from a home that is straight for longer than thirty minutes; there is always something on the floor when toddlers are present!

And last, the real test of your clutter quotient . . .

18. If the Lord called you home today, would you be horrified if your spouse accepted help from friends, relatives, or especially your mother-in-law to sort through your things?

Did you laugh at the thought of taking a clutter quiz because you already knew the answers? I hope the quiz didn't produce too much bad news for you, but no matter the result, it isn't too late.

Functional Neatness

How do you achieve the balance that's best for your home? I call that balance *functional neatness*—the comfortable place between (1) an obsessive neatness demanded by a mother who doesn't allow for a mess of any kind and is overworked trying to maintain that standard, and (2) slovenly conduct by family members. The measure for functional neatness is *neat enough to be peaceful and messy enough to be happy*. When there's stress in your home because you function in either extreme, it's hard to relax and concentrate on the important things. Either you're running a boot camp that makes the family miserable, or you're fighting messes that divert you and family members from joyous living.

Determine with your spouse and older children what works for your family. I learned that dirty floors really bothered my husband, but he didn't especially notice other things that were not done. When there was no time to do everything, I cleaned the floors first.

The goal isn't neatness in itself, although reasonable neatness produces a more pleasing, productive, and peaceful place. It's easier for you to maintain order when you de-clutter; everyone in the family functions better. However, your true aim is to rid your life of detrimental clutter of all kinds. You will free yourself to produce fruit in important things *and* to teach your children good stewardship of possessions and time.

God is not a God of disorder but of peace.

—1 Corinthians 14:33

The Good News

I promised you good news, and you may be wondering when I get to that part! The good news is that there's a difference between destructive, chaotic clutter and what I call "happy messes." If you homeschool, have a family who loves to learn, have hobbies, or just live life, you will have to deal with messes, even creative messes.

Knowing the difference in clutter or junk and happy messes is important. To determine the difference, ask yourself these questions:

1. Is the mess temporary?
2. Is it a mess created because of a project that will have a definite beginning and ending?
3. Is it serving a useful purpose for body, mind, or spirit?
4. Is it ministering to or serving the people around you?
5. Is it being *currently* used and enjoyed?

If you can answer *yes* to these questions, you have a happy mess. If not, you can't classify the mess as useful clutter no matter how much you rationalize. Creative messes are temporary or useful; determine if that applies to your various piles.

> # One of the advantages of being disorderly is that one is constantly making exciting discoveries.
>
> —A. A. Milne, *http://en.thinkexist.com*

All of us are sometimes blind to our personal clutter and junk. We tenaciously cling to our treasures while we see others' clutter much quicker, especially the clutter that belongs to our family members. Perhaps you haven't identified your clutter yet; decisions are difficult. It would be simple to throw out others' junk, but making choices about your clutter is harder. This is the starting place, but often it seems impossible to get past this hurdle in order to solve the problem. It's easier when you decide that you *must* take action. John 15:2 says that God prunes every branch that doesn't bear fruit so it will be more fruitful. Submitting yourself to God so He can prune you might involve the pruning of your clutter and junk.

Junk Journey

You are about to embark on a junk journey. It *is* a journey rather than a destination because junk continues to invade your home even after you manage a grand clean-out. The problems that junk and clutter cause aren't worth the price you pay: clutching useless clutter or activities pulls you down, stresses you out, and complicates your life. You'll be amazed at how many of those problems evaporate when the junk disappears.

When is the best time to de-clutter? School break, whether it's summer or otherwise, is a great time; but don't wait until then if it will be a long while before you take a break. See chapter 7 for options, but the earliest possible day and time that you can temporarily suspend other commitments is the best time. If you wait, you'll lose your resolve. In fact, the best day is the day before the garbage truck comes. It's easier to forget about your junk when it's gone for good!

Since you probably have more to de-clutter than you can finish in one day—I hope that isn't too much of an understatement—list areas on paper or computer that need your attention: the hall closet, kitchen cabinets and drawers, the medicine cabinet, your bedroom closet, and so forth. You can number these by priority if you wish, or you can choose from the list and check them off as you complete them. Don't be a slave to the list; it's only a guide and reminder. Post your list in a place where you will see it often.

> It is better to take many small
> steps in the right direction than
> to make a great leap forward only
> to stumble backward.
>
> —Old Chinese Proverb, *http://en.thinkexist.com*

Where do you begin when you are up to your earlobes? Every journey begins with the first step. You have made up your mind that you will take control of the stuff in your life, and you are ready to move toward the solution. Right? So let's clean a closet.

As you read, you can mentally clean a closet or any other area of your home. Then I encourage you to use these principles on the real thing. The principles apply to any area you need to de-junk: closets, cabinets, drawers, refrigerator, automobile, kids' rooms, purse, and even the garage. Nevertheless, I encourage you not to start with the garage; you may never come out! We'll look at paper clutter in chapters 5 and 6, since paper presents unique problems and challenges for everyone.

Small is Better

If you're overwhelmed, choose one small area that bothers you the most. That may be an overstuffed kitchen drawer, a small cabinet or shelf, a medicine cabinet, or a couple of dresser drawers. De-junk an area that you can finish in a short time, thus gaining a sense of accomplishment. That will encourage you to continue your junk journey.

Concentrate on the area you've chosen and don't go to another until you have finished where you started. It's easy to be distracted by *all* the areas you need to tackle as you work on the current one. This step is especially important if you have a compulsive personality or if you are a right-brain-dominant person. Stay with it until you're finished.

Those of you with a competitive streak may want to set a timer and race the clock. When normal interruptions happen, deal with them and go right back to your task. If you have set aside longer than a couple of hours to de-clutter, take a short break after an hour for a cup of tea or fifteen minutes on the front porch talking with your children, and then resume your clean-out. Keep reminding yourself of the outcome; picture what the closet or drawer will look like when it's restored to order.

Gather Containers

Containers are wonderful! Just think, God chose to contain who we really are—our being and personality—in containers called our bodies. You may wish for a better wrapping, but what is in that container is the special person God made you. Your Creator has chosen to dwell in that container with you as well (Ephesians 3:17; Romans 8:11). Doesn't that make containers rather special?

> Now we have this treasure in clay jars,
> so that this extraordinary power may
> be from God and not from us.
>
> —*2 Corinthians 4:7*

Containers also make great peace treaties between you and your children. Parents have the prerogative of choosing how many containers a child may use for his possessions, but the child may keep whatever treasures he likes as long as they are contained. That is, unless one of those possessions grows green slime or gives off toxic fumes! More about that in chapter 4.

Use containers in your closet to help corral your things. Even a mess put into a container looks better. Belts put into an inexpensive plastic wash pan and set on a shelf look nicer than belts falling all over the closet. Stacked plastic bins hold small items and look neater. You don't have to spend hundreds to make your closet look almost like the ads you see in magazines for closet organizers. Your closet may never look exactly like those dream closets, but you will be able to find what you need more quickly and easily.

Gather containers prior to beginning your de-clutter time. You'll need at least three containers for your job, plus a couple of trash bags. Depending on the size of the de-clutter location, you can use boxes or large plastic trash bags. For example, if your task is to clean out a kitchen drawer, you may only need three small boxes and the kitchen trash can beside you. The garage would require larger containers and more than three. The need for at least three containers will be evident in just a moment.

Don't Rearrange

You may have attempted a closet clean-out in the past by pulling out a few things and trying to rearrange the remainder. You already know that method doesn't work well. Remember your goal—to rid yourself and your family of detrimental clutter, not just to straighten your closet.

In your chosen area (drawer, closet, etc.), begin by emptying the area. That can be a frightening thought, but please don't panic or close the book right now! There are many advantages to starting with an empty space. Now is the time to clean it, wipe it, wash it, vacuum it, and even paint it, if needed. You have a beautiful canvas on which to work, somewhat like painting the background of a lovely picture. It forms the base of your finished result. Besides, by pulling everything out of the area, you may find things you thought you'd lost!

A professional organizer once disagreed with me about emptying a closet to de-junk it. I'm not a "professional." I'm a mom just like you. If the thought of emptying your closet is daunting, please do it your way. The goal is the result. I've rearranged too many closets without results, so I vote for a clean slate to end clutter effectively. If you are a mother of a toddler, you may have limited time to work on a project and may choose to do half a closet at a time. Perhaps you could tackle the garage one section at a time as well. Whatever method you choose, the advantages of emptying the space outweigh the disadvantages when you are de-cluttering most areas.

Decisions, Decisions, Decisions

About now you are at least mentally staring at the pile that came out of your closet and asking yourself how it all fit in that space! There's no turning back now; you have to go forward. This part is hard, and it is at this point in the past that you may have faltered. You must be ruthless with yourself. Decision-making is the most difficult part of de-cluttering, and you are called to make many, many small decisions.

One desperate mom admitted that she had repeatedly failed to get her house in order because she would stare at the items she knew she needed to deal with and just close the door or drawer. She needed help making those decisions since they were overwhelming her.

> My grace is sufficient for you, for power is perfected in weakness.
>
> —*2 Corinthians 12:9*

I recommend the buddy system for those who need that help. A spouse *can* be of assistance under some circumstances, but at other times the spouse is part of the problem. You may need a reliable friend who can say, "Why in the world are you keeping *that*?" and still be your friend after helping you with a cleanout. Maybe you only need a boost getting started, and once your friend assists you with the big messy closet, you can proceed from that point. Don't be ashamed to ask for help. Remember, it's easier to see other people's clutter than your own. You might be a lifesaver to a friend in need as well.

Sort, Sort, Sort

Let's start on the pile. Now you use the three containers I mentioned. Label each of the three (or more than one per category, if needed) as follows:

- Necessary (needed to function)
- Nice (useful to have but not used often)
- Never (junk, broken, unrepairable, outdated, ugly, useless, or no longer needed)

Everything in your pile goes into one of the three containers labeled with the three categories. Nothing floats around without a decision.

Necessary items are the things that you are *currently* using, that *currently* fit, that you are *currently* enjoying, and that you *must* have to function in your home. These things go into your container marked Necessary while you continue sorting and until you return them to their place later. Be selective. Necessary items don't include clothes that you hope to fit into someday, annually used items, keepsakes, gadgets that are too much trouble to use, duplicates, things you dislike, broken items, and anything that you haven't used in the past year.

Nice items are things that you enjoy and that are useful, but you don't need in order to survive. You would *not* take these items with you if you were packing light to move to a foreign country—or evacuating for a hurricane as we have to do in my area! Things that qualify for the Nice category include such items as those used annually, holiday decorations, special and company dishes, special collections, or unusual equipment for special jobs. (Does anyone own or use a floor polisher anymore?) This stage is dangerous territory since you can rationalize your stuff easily. The criterion is the same as the Necessary category: you should use them, need them, or enjoy them at least once a year. You can store many Nice items in a closet or on a shelf that is out of your home's usual daily traffic areas rather than in places you frequently use. Put these into your container marked Nice until you are finished sorting.

Last, but really first in importance, are items that belong in the Never category. You face three options with these items. You can throw them away, give them away, or sell them; but the essential thing to remember about these is that you are getting rid of them in some way! They are either not usable or you never use them. You can elect to use three containers marked Never—Give Away, Never—Sell, and Never—Toss. A large trash bag works for the discard junk in the Toss category.

You should toss items immediately if they are broken, unrepairable, useless, the remaining one of a pair that you haven't seen in a long while, or otherwise not fit for human use. As you sort, put those items in a trash bag and THROW THEM AWAY NOW! Don't give them a second thought or entertain the idea that you might use them someday. Yes, there really are people who replace a broken part with a new one and keep the broken one! Just think of it as tossing your stress. I know that some of you have gone back to the trash can and dug out an item you just threw away. I've done it on occasion myself. Don't do it this time. Remember, the garbage truck comes tomorrow, and you will be a free person!

You may decide to give some Never items away. As you sort, add items that are usable by others but not by you to the container marked Never or Never—Give Away. Maybe you can pass along to others any repairable item that you know you won't repair or any item that you no longer need. This sharing gives you an opportunity to teach your children generosity. Explain that you are giving to others when you donate to a charity since children may not make the connection by merely seeing you deliver bags or boxes to a location.

> ## The one who gives to the poor will not be in need.
>
> *—Proverbs 28:27*

Remember that these items are ones you don't want or need any longer. Treat them like the items you throw away; deliver the giveaways as quickly as possible to your chosen charity. You might plan a special trip for the same afternoon or the day following your clean-out. A friend says she rewards herself and the kids with ice cream after they take a load to a charity.

While sorting, if you discover an item that you know you or your spouse will repair and put to good use, put that item in an attractive basket, box, or other container and put the container in a prominent place—on a kitchen bar, in the laundry room, or elsewhere—for repair soon. By using a repair container, you'll solve the plight of the lost part by containing the item and its parts until you, your spouse, or your older child can make the repair. If the item is too large to go into your container, write the name of the item on a slip of paper, note where you stored the item and its parts, and put the paper in the container to serve as a reminder that it needs attention. If you use a pretty basket or box, your repairables can sit in view without being an eyesore. If a repair can wait, it is easier to get tools, glue, or tape out to restore several items at one time than to stop every time something needs a little glue or a screw.

The third option for discard items is to sell them. Oh, the infamous yard sale! Are you a yard-sale-goer or a yard-sale-giver? If you need to dispose of useful items and you don't want to give them away, you can place an ad in the newspaper or have a yard sale. Remember that these are items you are getting rid of for good. If you have a sale with a friend, resist the temptation to swap treasures. To help your resolve, arrange for pickup or take your leftover items to a charity immediately following the sale or by the next day. Box up the leftovers after the sale and put the containers in the car or on the porch for pickup. If you are tempted to fish some of the things out of the boxes, remind yourself that if it had sold, you wouldn't have it so you don't need it now.

If you are overwhelmed with the volume of clutter to sort, you may need to take the entire process in easier steps. First sort simply by Keep, Toss (true junk), and Undecided. This process requires that you go back and sort the undecided items, but it may get you started if the job seems enormous. The decisions may be simpler after that initial clean-out.

Location, Location, Location

By now you are almost to the end of the pile and have placed the items in the proper containers or put them in a trash bag. Your closet (or other area) is clean and ready for you to return the appropriate items.

Now is the time to evaluate whether an item should go back into this location. So many times in our rush we open a door or drawer and stuff something in without considering the best place to put it. The general rule is to store an item in a place that is near where you most frequently use it. If your vacuum is stored in the entry closet and you have to transport it to the bedrooms where the only carpet in the house is located, move it. If you live in a two-story house, buy duplicates of anything you can afford—cleaning supplies, tools, and even vacuum cleaners. Store school supplies close to the area where the children study. Move the games to a cabinet in the family room if that's where you play games. If an item is inconvenient to put away, family members will be tempted to put it down anywhere with a promise to "put it away later." More clutter!

If an item from your clean-out area doesn't belong back in that area, put it in its appropriate Necessary or Nice box and continue working. After you return all items to the area, you can move the things that belong elsewhere to a better spot. Don't stop in the middle of your work to look for a place to store that item. Some glassy-eyed moms have wandered off and never returned! See chapter 7 for more ideas.

Dispensations and Exceptions

Yes, your junk journey includes exceptions. Your mind, as you read, probably registered some, since emotions wind tightly around our stuff. This dilemma only increased when our family began homeschooling. What do you do with the exploding volcano that your children worked so hard on for the science fair? Where do you store (or *do* you store) the giant Roman city they built while studying ancient Rome?

Watch out and be on guard against all greed because one's life is not in the abundance of his possessions.

—*Luke 12:15*

The emotional tricks your heart plays when you start your junk journey are real. The thought of getting rid of some objects, regardless of their current usability, seems to rip away a part of you. You feel that you would lose part of your life or betray someone if you were to discard certain items. Even though we live in a throwaway world, it seems like a sin if we toss something that *might* be useful. Have you experienced that feeling? Remember, this is a junk journey not a guilt trip!

As you sort, if you find yourself staring at items that you have no idea what to do with but you can't bring yourself to get rid of, there are some remedies. Ask yourself these questions:

1. *How long have I had it?* Remember the one-year rule I mentioned. If you have not used it in a long time and it could be useful to others, put it in the give-away box; you won't regret blessing someone else. If you still can't bring yourself to discard it because of sentimental reasons, put it in your PASS box (keep reading).

2. *Is it disturbing my peace?* Maybe someone gave you a gift that you don't like or don't use, but you can't bring yourself to discard it or give it away. Keep in mind that each time you see this object you have to deal with the same feeling again. Everyone receives gift mistakes, so get rid of it now or pass it on to someone else. A friend of mine calls that regifting. Your peace is worth more than the recurring irritation.

3. *Does it deserve a place in my life?* Things are only useful when they don't hinder relationships with people and when they help you enjoy and serve the people around you. I'm not talking about strictly utilitarian things; beautiful things and sentimental things count—to a limit— as well.

4. *What will happen if I don't have this item any longer?* If you can answer, "nothing," let it go now. Often we fear that we will need it again, but the truth is that when we have so much clutter and junk, we don't even *think* about some items, and we certainly never *use* them. Most things are replaceable, and the freedom from minor mistakes in judgment is worth more than the cost of replacing an item or two if you need it.

If you struggle with these things, you need a dispensation—a PASS box (PArting is Sweet Sorrow). While sorting, when you come across those irresistible items that tug at your heart but are useless to you or anyone else, put them in one box. Tape it up and with a black marker write PASS and the date on it large enough to see. Store the box in a place where you can retrieve it in six months. If you are very sentimental, you may need longer. When the time has passed, don't open the box! If you no longer remember what is in the box, toss it out. If you don't remember what is there, you won't miss it when it's gone—let it pass away quietly without fanfare. If the pain of tossing it is still present, follow these instructions: leave it closed; put it back on the shelf; repeat the above in another six months; and this time toss it!

Saving Sentiments

Our fourth and last son was born at home in 1979. It was a special and meaningful time, and I am grateful that I was able to have that experience. We had a king-size bed then, but when replacement time came for that bed, I had a hard time getting rid of it. It represented a positive and special memory, and I cried when we disposed of it.

Why are those sentimental items hard to part with? What is it that we really desire by keeping a certain object? The inanimate object represents part of our life, and we enjoy the special memories that flood back into our hearts when we see it. The older I get, the more I like those warm fuzzies! However, reality suggests that we can't keep everything. We would need to double the size of our homes and storage places if we kept every memento that enters our lives.

I'm grateful for the gift of photography. By taking pictures of those special things, we keep what we really want—something to remind us of the memory, the relationship, or the event. A picture is a good alternative to saving the item that takes up valuable space. Try setting up a display in your home for the school projects your children create. A card table in a corner of our family room works well, but find your own special spot. Allow the project to be on display for an agreed-upon length of time, and take a picture of the children with their special creation, trophy, or object. The display can be an encouragement to the children when visitors come to your home and see their treasures. A good school project, created by each child, is a personal school yearbook of pictures and souvenirs from the school year. It gives the child a way to preserve those special memories without the clutter.

Allow your children to choose their special papers and drawings and keep them in a large, flat art folder or a box. As they add more things, filling the folder or container, have them choose items to remove and discard or to put into their scrapbooks.

One friend preserved a treasured memento in a unique way. She possessed an old fishing creel, which is a wicker basket used to hold fish as an angler catches them, that belonged to her now-deceased grandfather. The weaving in the bottom was torn and tattered, rendering the creel of no use. She was close to her grandfather, and she couldn't bear to part with the creel; however, it was collecting dust and taking up space in the garage. One day she brought it into her house, cleaned it up, and put a piece of heavy cardboard inside the bottom. She then propped open the lid and placed dried flowers in the creel, relocating the new decoration beside her fireplace. There she could see the cherished keepsake daily and enjoy the warm memories of her grandfather. Rather than store special treasures out of sight, look for practical ways to use or display them. You will turn clutter into useful treasure.

Homeschooling moms typically become specialists at turning outings or vacations into field trips. You have probably learned to combine Dad's work trips, vacations, camping trips, and even trips to the grocery store into learning experiences. Often those trips, especially long car journeys, generate souvenirs, books, or other materials that accumulate. Containers are useful friends when you travel. Take along plenty of zip-type plastic bags and carry a plastic crate to hold such necessities as paper towels, wet wipes, a couple of small umbrellas, bags of nutritious snacks, and other needed items. Give each child a drawstring bag that is big enough to accommodate puzzles, items that are suitable for quiet car entertainment, coloring books, and colored pencils. Remember that crayons melt in the hot car and produce more misery than you want to deal with on a trip. Plastic boxes labeled with each child's name and with snapable lids work well, too. The rule while riding should be that when children take an item from the bag or box, they have to return it before they remove another item. This system requires some supervision, and it doesn't work perfectly (unless you are a mom with perfect kids), but it can prevent items from tumbling out of the car or van each time you stop.

Practice yourself, for heaven's sake, in little things; and thence proceed to greater.

—Epictetus, *Little Things*

To tame the volume while traveling and when you arrive home, let children choose what they want to take along, within the limits you set and with the stipulation that their items fit in the bag or box. In addition, tuck in a couple of surprises they won't see until you are on the road. Limit souvenir purchases by either a dollar amount or by quantity to keep the clutter from growing. More about children and their mementos in chapter 4.

May I offer a defense for grandparents here? On numerous occasions grandparents have asked me to convey information to their adult children. Please retrieve your stuff that is stored at your parents' house. They will bless you for it. Your childhood home isn't a public storage facility, and you will ease possible family tension by claiming your possessions. When your family arrives for a visit, show respect and consideration by caring for and keeping organized the grandparents' space. Pick up and put away items that have been used or played with during your visit. Perhaps you could even take dirty sheets and towels to the laundry room. Use the List Minder on the CD, if necessary, to ensure you have gathered all your family possessions when it's time to leave. Everyone accidentally leaves behind an item on occasion, but if your family habitually leaves a trail of belongings at each visit, you probably are also leaving hesitant grandparents who love to see you but wish you would make the stay a little easier for them.

Wise Warning from the Word

You may have new enthusiasm for clearing your clutter and jettisoning your junk, but your family may not share your exuberance. It's easy to go overboard in your new zeal for bringing order out of chaos.

I recall one of my determined clean-out sprees several years ago. My husband had constructed a small, wooden step stool in his college days, and it had migrated to become one of our family possessions. It wasn't useful for the children to use in stepping up to a sink or other area. It tipped easily, causing wounds that I had bandaged frequently, and it was too low to sit on. I had tried numerous ways to use it, including as a plant stand, but it really just floated around the house, not of much use to anyone.

Because he hadn't shown any particular attachment to the stool, the next yard sale seemed like the perfect opportunity to rid us of the loathed item. Out it went. Later, when my husband missed it, I told him what I had done. He wasn't very pleased with me for selling his treasure, and I had to apologize and confess that I was wrong to get rid of it without asking him. It was, after all, his stool.

From that embarrassing incident I learned a valuable lesson about respecting family members' possessions. God emblazed Philippians 2:3–4 on my heart: "Do nothing out of rivalry or conceit, but in humility consider others as more important than yourselves. Everyone should look out not [only] for his own interests, but also for the interests of others."

While there should be guidelines in a family, there must also be flexibility. Be a good example for your children with the use and maintenance of possessions while you train them to take care of and properly use what they have. This training comes with practice on their part and patience on your part. Clear the destructive clutter in your home and teach your children to do so, but give family members some latitude with limits for their own possessions. Prevent messes every possible place you can and teach your children to be sharers rather than savers (in the destructive, hoarding sense of savers), but expect that your home won't look perfect all the time.

Clutter costs in numerous ways: buying it, cleaning it, maintaining it, storing it, protecting it, and moving it. The benefits of clearing clutter exceed the time and energy to do so, and once you are free from the restrictions of clutter, you will not want to go back.

It is easier to *keep* a home clutter free than it is to *make* it clutter free. No one, even naturally organized people, will do it perfectly; but once you have conquered the piles, maintaining order requires effort. Schedule a time for quick pickups in your simple, basic schedule and allow for a thorough clean-out about once a year.

In the end, when you (mother) accept your position as a woman of God and see your home as your workplace, you honor the Lord. Your home will speak to the hurt and dying world that *here* it is different; your peaceful, restful, harmonious, and happy haven for family and guests will be a witness to the world, a witness that speaks of the simplicity of faith in Christ. Isn't that worth throwing out some clutter in your junk journey?

STOP Stop, Look, Think

Direction—Where Are You Going?

1. Are possessions out of control in your home? Do you have too much stuff that is limiting your life in any way? Decide with your family, including the children if they are old enough, the level of functional neatness you can maintain together.

2. Explain to your family the difference between clutter and happy messes. Help them judge the difference when there is a mess—yours or theirs.

3. Where do you need to direct your attention to begin clearing the clutter? List areas of your home that need de-cluttering.

4. Post your list and choose one small place to start. Choose a day to begin and gather containers you need. Enlist help from family members who are able to help. Work together until you have de-cluttered all the areas on your list.

5. Do you need to use the buddy system when you de-clutter? Ask a friend, spouse, or older child to help you. If other family members are more resolved than you are, praise them for that talent and use their ability to recognize junk to de-clutter your home.

Devotion—What Are You Thinking?

1. List relationships that clutter is hindering. How is the clutter affecting those relationships?

2. Confess to the Lord any area where you may need to repent: clutching your possessions too tightly, putting yourself above others in the family, being lazy concerning the order of your home, not trusting the Lord to provide for you and thereby holding on to many things out of fear, not training your children to take care of their possessions, and so forth. Ask Him to forgive you and to help you overcome the things that you confessed.

3. Pray for wisdom if family members are large contributors to the clutter problem in your home. Ask Him how to deal with them, and ask Him for patience as you train your children. Prayerfully decide how to discuss the problem with your spouse while sharing why you want your home clutter-free and orderly. Come to your spouse without accusations and in the spirit of humility.

4. Read the following Scriptures and meditate on them: Philippians 2:1–4; Luke 12:13–34; and 1 Timothy 6:6–8.

Notes

Chapter 4
Teaching Children Life Skills

W hile browsing in a stationary and office supply store, I found a line of note cards, key rings, notepads, and other products bearing the same cartoon illustration and slogan. The picture was of a worn and harried mother standing at the kitchen sink with a baby on her hip and a toddler at her side tugging on her skirt. Her disheveled hair and the desperate look on her face told the story. Under the picture was the caption, "Motherhood is not for wimps!" I laughed aloud at the familiar scenario. Sympathy sells, and I imagine some enterprising American mother was cashing in on her plight; only an experienced mom could have painted the picture so accurately.

I'm grateful God gave me children, and I don't believe they are a curse. In fact, they are an amazing blessing. Nevertheless, there was a time when I didn't think so. Because I'm a baby boomer, I have twice as many children as I thought I would have; and because the Lord redeemed my life, I have half as many as I wish I had. But no matter how many children God gives us, it isn't an easy task raising them to be mature, functioning adults who love the Lord.

Mom, you have chosen a labor-intensive job. Raising children and cleaning up after them is always a challenge. If you have boys, you also wash the soap when you clean the bathroom! As a mom, you may take your knocks and bruises from society, from politicians, and maybe even from a well-meaning mother or mother-in-law telling you that you are wasting your talents at home. But *you* know it's God's call on your life to educate and disciple your children at home.

If I could ask you what your greatest aspiration is for your children, you might say something like, "I want to raise well-balanced adults who love the Lord and other people and who will go out into the world to fulfill their particular calling from God—adults who can effectively manage their homes and families and be of service to those around them." That heartfelt expression is most Christian parents' desire for the children God has given them, but that outcome requires training. Since habits precede the understanding of principles, we must train our children in the virtues that make selflessness and self-control possible. Teaching life skills is a powerful means of doing so.

> Sons are indeed a heritage from the LORD, children, a reward.
>
> —*Psalm 127:3*

You may be familiar with the verses in Deuteronomy 6:6–9 that tell us to teach our children as we go about our everyday lives—as we rise up, sit down, and walk by the way. However, in homeschooling we can become so focused on academics, for fear we won't give our children a good education, that we forget to emphasize the sometimes mundane life skills they need to survive and thrive. Children don't absorb these skills by osmosis.

Occasionally the dailiness of life causes us to skip the training in favor of waiting until later. It's easier to close the bedroom door on a mess or do the chores ourselves than take twice as long to teach a child *again* to do it. Perhaps you enjoy teaching academics to your children, but you would rather not face the potential tug-of-war in getting them to work. You *teach* your children's minds, but you *train* their will, which is more difficult.

My oldest son taught me a wonderful lesson about how important it is to teach children, even boys, basic life skills, and how easy it is to overlook some of the smaller, more familiar things. Following high school graduation, he enlisted in the navy and left home that summer. About six weeks after his departure, I received a precious letter from him telling me how much he appreciated all I had taught him, how valuable those lessons were, and how much more he understood now that he was on his own. It was the kind of letter every mother cherishes, and I was heartened that I had done at least a few things right on the parenting path. At the bottom of the letter he added this postscript: "Mom, you didn't teach me to iron!" How, with my embarrassing ironing experience, could I have overlooked *that*?

You can probably guess that my younger sons have since learned to iron.

A number of years ago, while a group of homeschool moms gathered at a meeting to discuss the trials and tribulations of homeschooling, one mother spoke up and said with a smile, "I could really get into this homeschooling thing—if it weren't for the kids." We all laughed at her remark, but she was right: Because children can be uncooperative, this parenting gig simply isn't as easy as we would like.

It Begins with You

When I was a young mother, I tried to ignore the fact that the starting point in teaching my sons life skills began with me. My own life was the quintessential example of the necessity of such training, and I knew teaching them would make an enormous difference in their ability to function in the future. Nevertheless, I felt handicapped and had to learn as I taught *them*.

If you have weaknesses in homemaking skills, diligently continue to improve in those areas. Because your children are watching and they learn what they see, it's important they see you try a task, possibly fail, and try again while you demonstrate a healthy and prayerful attitude. They learn discipline when they see you exhibit discipline in your life. If you walk away from chores, put chores off indefinitely, or act as though slovenly habits or an unclean house don't matter, they will establish the same habits. In fact, family chores are one of the most effective vehicles to prepare them for life. However, you do your children a disservice when the focus is more on the chore than on the character that mastering and completing the chore builds into their lives.

> ## We cannot teach our children to praise God for whatever He sets their hands to do, until we have learned that ourselves.
>
> —Terry Dorian, *Anyone Can Homeschool*

Your children quickly catch your attitudes. If you display a complaining spirit or dump the chores you don't like to do on them or excessively make an older child your "go-for," resentment quickly builds. Conversely, if you maintain a cheerful attitude while going about everyday tasks, you communicate that what you are doing is important and has meaning. You convey that these tasks are a vital part of a functioning household, that a family works together to accomplish these tasks, and that they are to serve one another with a kind and cheerful spirit.

Life Skills

As I sorted out the things I needed to teach my children, I felt overwhelmed. They needed to acquire many practical skills, and lessons in character development were an additional and important by-product of their training. They should learn to clean their rooms, but learning respect for the possessions God provides was equally important. I began by asking these two questions about each skill I needed to teach: If I don't teach ____, will the lack of that knowledge be harmful or a hindrance to them later in life? How can learning this skill be a vehicle to teaching a greater character lesson? I divided skills into three major areas:

- Functional neatness (*neat enough to be peaceful and messy enough to be happy*—chapter 3)
- Priorities and wise use of time
- Record-keeping and finances

Functional Neatness

I guarantee that your definition of neatness will not match your children's definitions! Once you have determined the balance for your home, the more difficult part begins—enforcing it! Train your children early. Yes, I know it takes longer for you to teach children to do a job than for you to do it yourself; but the long-term rewards for all of you are worth the investment of time.

Time stays long enough for anyone who will use it.

—Leonardo Da Vinci, *http://quotations.about.com*

Our family experienced the fruit of training in an interesting way when I fell down a flight of metal warehouse stairs and broke both feet the week prior to moving into a new home. Full recovery took sixteen weeks, and I spent a great deal of time on our sofa giving directions and homeschooling. The younger two sons were teens at the time, and it would have been difficult for our family to function well without their able help with everything from unpacking the moving boxes to doing the laundry to fixing the meals to cleaning the house. When they were young, it never occurred to me while I was teaching them to clean a bathroom that they would have to assume such a big responsibility later. I was grateful I had taught them how to do those things!

Young two- or three-year-old children are eager to help and to please Mommy and Daddy. This age is an ideal time to begin their training, and functional neatness is the place to start. Young children can understand that they are part of the family and can be helpers as they grow into the abstract ideas of time and priorities.

A friend shared the analogy she uses to illustrate this training technique to her children: Each family member is like a wheel on the family van. Conveniently, there are four in her family. If the four wheels don't work together, the van can't go anywhere. If one tire is low and not doing its share, it affects the others. If one tire is flat or quits, the entire van comes to a stop, and someone has to correct or fix the tire. Her children understood the word picture right away.

The small tasks you teach now build a base for future life skills and help your children in their academic study. When children do simple chores, they learn to think in an orderly way. They can learn to put away toys when they are finished playing with them, to make their beds with assistance, to set the table, to put the clean silverware in the drawer in the proper place, to sort their socks and to fold clothes, even if it's just the washcloths. Rather than praise children only for the good job (the bed looks nice), praise them also for the character trait they display. For example, "You are a diligent worker to finish your job," or, "You were patient when you tried again to do a good job." It takes patience and time to teach children, but let them work right along with you in your daily tasks.

Teach a youth about the way he should go; even when he is old he will not depart from it.

—*Proverbs 22:6*

Simple Rules

A number of years ago a father who attended one of my conference workshops related this story to me rather sheepishly: "I have a confession to make. I'm wearing very uncomfortable shoes, and I want to tell you why." He told how his family had developed a habit of taking off their shoes when they came inside the house to keep the carpet clean, but they left them scattered everywhere rather than putting them away. The problem had escalated to an unmanageable degree and affected family relationships when tempers flared over lost shoes. Anytime the family wanted to go somewhere, at least one family member had to look for shoes, and the dad would become impatient and irritable when the family was late.

The dad admitted he was one of the worst offenders, and the Lord had shown him that in order to train his family he would have to be a good example. He called a family meeting at which they established some permissible places for shoes—the closet, on a mat beside the door, and so forth. When family members found shoes in improper places, they were allowed to confiscate the errant pair and sentence it to a penalty box for an agreed upon time limit. If the impounded shoes were the owner's Sunday shoes and the time limit included Sunday, the person had to wear some other pair to church.

This dad reported that, for fear of losing a favorite pair of shoes, family members were improving; but they weren't perfect yet, including Dad. He had lost his favorite pair of walking shoes and was wearing a less comfortable pair to the conference. His children loved finding a pair of Dad's shoes out of their proper place, which also reminded them of their own shoes. These children were learning responsibility for their belongings, but they were learning something else equally as valuable. They witnessed a wise dad who was willing to admit his weaknesses and become vulnerable in order to reform his bad habit and teach his children.

As this father discovered, *simple* rules are more effective and are easier to maintain while teaching a skill or habit to children. You, also, may find that a lost and found department in your home is effective. If you struggle with uncooperative children and home maintenance, begin by determining a few simple and enforceable rules necessary to operate your home. An acceptable level of functional neatness makes for a smoother running home. List three or four rules at a time and post them where all family members can view them, using pictures for nonreaders. You might include the penalty for violating the rule as well. Since your rules will be different from another family's rules, choose the important ones for your household.

Gaining Cooperation

Setting the rules is the easy part. The most important yet difficult part is sticking to the rules. Without follow-up and consequence, you will only waste your time and teach your children that they don't have to do what you tell them to do. If you instruct your son to clean the bathroom, he doesn't do it, and you don't follow-up to see that he did, he will learn that he doesn't have to clean the bathroom or obey you. Mom and Dad, you must support each other in sticking to the rules, or the lessons the children learn will be opposite the ones you try to reinforce.

Work with your children and demonstrate the way to do a job. It's so tempting just to send them away to make the bed or sweep the floor without giving good instruction and without following up to see if they are doing well. While they're learning, they need follow-up soon after they have completed their chore to reinforce what they have done well and to receive corrective instruction when needed. If you have supervised well, you will be able to make fewer inspections as they get older. When you communicate to your children the things you expect, show them how to accomplish the tasks, and follow up to see what they have done, you'll gain greater cooperation. They may not love to clean the bathroom, but they'll know how and will thank you one day for the life lessons they learned while cleaning a toilet.

A habit cannot be tossed out the window; it must be coaxed down the stairs a step at a time.

—Mark Twain, *Little Things*

I found it most effective to establish a household work session when we all worked together for a set amount of time. Homeschool families I've seen who have cooperative and obedient children have a specific work time, study time, and play time—not impossibly scheduled by the clock but planned by a simple, basic routine based on segments of the day or situations. A friend who is a homeschooling single mom shared that "a more flexible approach works better for my family, so I plan in terms of a routine where things usually happen in a predictable sequence rather than a schedule where things happen at a certain time."

You accomplish more and everyone knows what you expect of them during these specific divisions. You may have a task to do while the children study or play; but generally, working, studying, and playing together produce more family unity, cooperation, and effectiveness in your home.

Your regular work time might be first thing in the morning before you start school or later in the day when you've finished some lessons. It may even be in the middle of the day for a break from school. Depending on your educational philosophy, young children under eight or nine years may need little or no formal instruction. Even if you give young children seat-type work, they need only about an hour a day. That arrangement provides an additional hour a day of cleanup when everyone takes part. The time doesn't matter as much as the consistency. If Dad is cooperative and able, he may help do larger tasks on the weekend while you maintain less demanding but necessary tasks during the week. Apply what you learned from chapter 2 to your family situation. Use the Master Household Routine and the Home Works Planner to help establish a family routine that works for you.

When I've questioned children about their biggest frustration with helping around the house, their most frequent response has been that parents require them to do a job without telling them how to do it. Then parents are not happy with them for doing the job poorly. This example tells parents how important it is to give their children good instruction. Remember my ironing?

She watches over the activities of her
household and is never idle.

—*Proverbs 31:27*

Your Child's Room

I've found the appropriate Scripture to use when you face the challenge of teaching children to clean their rooms: "What should I say—Father, save me from this hour?" (John 12:27). When my sons attended college, I realized many parents must have simply closed the bedroom door and had no rules for functional neatness. Have you ever peeked into college dorm rooms? Closing the door doesn't solve the long-term problem.

Apply those simple, enforceable rules again for cleaning and maintaining a child's room. Both you and your children benefit if they know what you expect. Clearly define a clean room for them. List the things you plan to inspect, then post the list or chart on the closet door, the wall, or on a bulletin board in the child's room. (See the Clean Room Chart on the CD.)

A clean-bathroom chart posted in the bathroom or lists posted in each room of the house might be more effective than a central chore chart, usually posted in the kitchen. This list can be a simple reference list for your children to consult or it can be a weekly list for them to check as they complete each chore. If you laminate the list and use an erasable marker, they can erase it at the end of the week and start over the following week. Multiple children who share a room can use the same list or use their own.

See the accompanying CD for a sample chore chart (Household Minder) and a blank chart for your use, but make your own if you wish, based on your particular household and children. Whether you use this idea or one of your own, do use a chore chart of some type. It provides accountability for children and a guide for you to check their progress. If you use nothing, your work and their learning will be more difficult.

The Makeover

If you've neglected teaching your children how to clean their rooms or your children are young and you're beginning their training, you'll need to invest some time for a fresh start to avoid frustration for all of you.

Taming the volume of clutter in a child's room is the most helpful thing you can do to transform the room. Less is definitely better. The same clutter principles from chapter 3 apply in your children's rooms as well. In fact, room-cleaning time is a great opportunity to teach them those principles in the microcosm of their rooms. When toys for four boys in our home multiplied to an unwieldy mass, we all sorted toys into three groups: those to keep, those to give away, and those to store. We boxed the toys to store, labeled the box, and put it away in an accessible place. Several months later we brought the box out and allowed each child to choose anything he wanted from the box as long as he replaced it with some other toy. Then we put the box away again for several months. This rotation divided the volume and gave the boys something new and interesting to play with each time we rotated. For additional tips that apply to your children's rooms, see the CD.

When you involve children in the work and appearance of their rooms, they will more likely look forward to helping put their rooms in order. Before cleaning the room, plan a school craft day for them to decorate containers, letting them choose the decorations.

For the big clean-out, choose a time when you and your child are fresh and rested. Why do we tend to tackle projects that bother us the most when we feel the worst? Tell your child ahead of time that the two of you will do a makeover of his room on a certain day; it's best not to surprise him with the idea in order to prevent him from becoming defensive and fearful you will invade his special space. Once you've started, work until you have completed the job, doing it in one longer session or several shorter sessions. An unfinished job teaches your child something as well—that he doesn't have to finish what he starts.

Dads Can Help

Dads can help make a child's room easier to clean and keep clean. Together take a critical, child's-eye view of the room. Can your child reach the shelves and the closet bar to put away his things and hang up his clothes? Dad can lower the bar and build accessible shelves. You may end up with a shop class in the bargain if your child is old enough to help Dad, even if it is just assisting him by handing tools. At the least your child learns the names of the tools. If Dad isn't much of a carpenter, he can make simple shelves with sturdy boards and blocks. Bought shelving is usually the most expensive option, but it works as well.

Be sure drawers in chests are easy to open and close. Dividers inside drawers can aid some children in keeping their things more organized, but for others the dividers are just a hindrance.

Think upward for storage. Dad can add shelves at the top of a closet to make storage room for infrequently used items or items such as extra pillows and blankets. A floor to ceiling pole made from a large wooden dowel or rod with hooks attached to it is a great place to hang coats, hats, or stuffed animals; and it takes up little floor space. Or hang a hammock of strong mesh material in a corner to capture stuffed animals.

Does your young child have a sturdy, one-step stool in his room and in the bathroom to reach those too-tall places? He's more likely to pick up and put away when he can reach things easily. Do you keep the laundry hamper where he undresses most often? For a long while I kept a large family hamper for everyone's clothes, but it was difficult for the children to use. I changed to smaller hampers for each child placed in their bedrooms. Clothes made it into the hampers more often, and each boy was responsible for bringing his hamper to the laundry room on wash day to sort clothes. Even a laundry basket filled with dirty clothes in the corner of a room looks better and teaches better habits than clothes strewn all over the floor and carelessly walked on. See things from your children's perspective to learn how you can improve the chances of their cooperation. Ask older children their opinions about what would help them keep their rooms clean. Parents learn a great deal when they just listen to their children.

Maintenance Training

The makeover is often the easy part. Now you must continue to teach good habits. Quick daily pickups and periodic cleanups are necessary to keep the room in good shape. Establish pickups and cleanups as part of your children's regular routine.

As my boys grew older, I had to remind myself to take the long view of a situation. Scripture teaches us that if we do not work, we do not eat (2 Thessalonians 3:10). Many of us see the advantage of having a family pet in order to teach our children responsibility, but who ends up feeding the pet? We feel sorry for our child and especially for the pet, so we give in and become the caregiver. One mom took a firmer approach as she put this scriptural principle to work in her home through the care of the family dog. She set a simple rule: the children were responsible for feeding the dog. If they forgot to feed the dog that day, they missed their supper that night. She wisely knew missing one meal would not harm her children and it wouldn't take many missed meals for them to remember to feed the dog.

Even a young man is known by his actions—by whether his behavior is pure and upright.

—*Proverbs 20:11*

I implemented the principle in a different way. My boys were forgetful, as children often are, about leaving all kinds of interesting things in their pockets when they tossed their pants into the laundry hamper (yes, in the hamper and not on the floor!). On wash day the items created a mess or even a disaster when we didn't check the pockets before washing. Repeated warnings didn't seem to help. A simple, enforceable rule was the answer.

I placed two containers on the shelf above the washer: a jar and a small plastic basket. When I checked pockets before washing and found money, it went into the jar as my pay for checking their pockets. Any small toy or other item went into the basket and the owner had to do an additional chore to earn it back. It was my option to throw away any item I deemed trash, and the forgetful boy lost his little treasure. In addition, if an item of clothing was not in the hamper when it was laundry time, I didn't wash it that day.

> Don't be alarmed when your children demonstrate inappropriate attitudes. Take that as an opportunity from the Lord to love your child in a very tangible way.
>
> —Debbie Strayer, *Gaining Confidence to Teach*

It was amazing how fast memories improved and how I found pockets empty more often than not! My mental picture of future daughters-in-law helped me stick to the rule so that my sons learned the lesson faster. Children do understand and begin to learn responsibility when parents are consistently firm. Hold your children accountable for the areas you know they are capable of handling. Don't demand perfection, but teach them to do their best at any job they do. An excellent memory verse for your children to learn is Proverbs 20:11.

Will your children accomplish these feats without flaw? Do you have to run a boot camp in your home? Of course not. Since life is messy and moves at a fast pace, you need to offer grace at times. Struggling children need you to come alongside them with help and encouragement, not condemnation. Nevertheless, they still need to learn the lessons before them, and they will do so more thoroughly with your assistance and firm patience. They won't learn if you do for them the things they can do for themselves, when they *should* do them for themselves. The principle that *people are more important than things, but things out of control hinder our relationships with people* especially seems to apply when we are teaching our children.

Time and Priorities

As your children grow older, they comprehend more about priorities and the wise use of time. Dinner table discussions can reinforce why you're teaching them life skills. Since children love to hear stories about their parents' or grandparents' childhood, tell them funny things that happened to you when you were learning how to do the routine things of life. Share the types of chores you did when you were young, how you struggled with a particular chore, or how you later suffered some consequence because you didn't know how to do a particular thing. Talk to your children as you go about the ordinary tasks of life—no lecture required. Your discussions can include productive ways to spend time, the most important priorities in your children's lives, and how to eliminate those things from life that don't fit your family priorities. When you include your children in discussions of family priorities, you teach them how to sort their thinking about these things.

As your children mature, they begin to grasp abstract ideas. Teach them simple goal-setting principles from chapter 2. Short-range goals can be an encouragement to them when they see results. Those goals help them see that a greater objective is possible and that there isn't time for everything in life they might possibly want to do. Choices are necessary in every area of their lives and in your family life. Help them sort through the choices to move closer to the things they are interested in for their future. Long-range goals help them see a wider picture of what they want in life. Help them understand that changing goals occasionally is normal.

Experience teaches your children a great deal about priorities and about life. Allow them room to make poor choices about their time and priorities, and then let them suffer the consequences. The frequent temptation is to bail them out when they're in an uncomfortable situation; however, they'll learn best when they learn within the safe environment of the family and deal with the consequences of their decisions.

[Children] understand that life is more than evaluation and that they are more than the sum of their test results.

—Debbie Strayer, *Gaining Confidence to Teach*

Record-keeping and Finances

The third major area of child training involves record-keeping and finances. Of the many things I didn't learn how to do before I left home, keeping a bank account and records was the most detrimental. I would have had fewer struggles if I had learned those skills.

At different ages children can begin to keep their own records and schedule. Most children need only a simple calendar hung in their room or in a place where they will see it often. More naturally organized children might enjoy a simple planner or an inexpensive PDA. They can record lesson times and dates, ball or music practice times, appointments, and special occasions. As appropriate, they can keep up with their individual school assignments or keep a journal. A place to record simple goals is helpful and can be encouraging as they see the progress they are making in an area. Let your child experiment with different methods to see which one is the most comfortable and helpful. An alternative is to keep a central family calendar with the basic family routine posted and allow children to record their relevant activities on that calendar. One friend keeps a dry-erase board hanging in an accessible place with prayer and praise lists and grocery and personal needs. Her children are responsible to record items on the board when they use the last, or almost last, of such items as animal food or personal toiletries; otherwise, needed items don't go on the grocery list for the next buying trip.

She says, "This has been helpful to me and a teaching tool for the children, helping them take on a bit of responsibility. If they need something but don't write it on the board, they are accountable to themselves."

Whatever methods you choose to train your children to keep up with their schedules and commitments or contribute to the household, will help build a consciousness of priorities and choices in their lives. It becomes a family matter to use time wisely, and they see your example. When they become responsible for their personal affairs, they begin to shift the load from Mom and Dad to themselves where, in the end, the responsibility belongs.

> Examine each standard or goal you accept for your family, considering whether or not it is God who is applying it to you.
>
> —Debbie Strayer, *Gaining Confidence to Teach*

Before children are old enough to open a bank account, but when they are old enough to understand the principles of a checking account, assemble a modified bank at home. Use checks and a register that are no longer useful, perhaps leftovers from changing banks or from moving to another address, or make some that look as genuine as possible.

Open a separate "account" for each of your children by letting them deposit money with you, the banker. Show them how to record deposits, write checks to withdraw money, and reconcile their accounts with a statement you prepare for each of them. Penalize them if they overdraw the account, and pay them interest if they keep a savings account. If you reproduce the experiences they would have with a real bank account, they will more likely be mature enough to handle an account when they are older.

The inevitable questions parents wrestle with concerning money are whether or not to give an allowance and how to administer it. Each family's situation and foundational view of money are so different it would be difficult to share specific advice that applies to everyone. However, I can share what we did in our family. It worked for us and taught the lessons we wanted taught.

To each child you might assign such specific maintenance chores as taking out the trash, keeping the bedroom and bathroom clean, helping with meal preparation, setting the table, cleaning the floor after meals, and so forth. Children are part of the family and help make the messes, so expect them to clean up those messes. Because they are part of the family, you can pay a small allowance not connected to specific chores. The allowance needs to be small enough that it doesn't supply them with everything they would like to have, especially when they are teens.

Require chores above their normal maintenance chores to earn extra money. We paid our sons well, usually close to the normal going rate for a particular job, since we would have to pay outside help anyway if it were something we planned to have done. They mowed the lawn, washed the cars, and made simple home repairs to earn extra money. Your list of "extras" might vary from ours. Older teens can hold jobs outside the home or start their own businesses for the pay and for the experience. One of my sons learned to juggle and ride a unicycle. He turned his fun into a prosperous clowning business for several years and even earned high school credit for performing arts.

Certain requirements applied to the money our boys earned and to their allowance. A minimum of 10 percent went to church, a minimum of 10 percent for savings, and then they could spend the remainder. They didn't have to divide gift money since it was usually in lieu of a purchased present from a grandparent. They could buy something with that gift money.

In relating to me that this is the same plan her family uses successfully, one friend said, "My children quickly saw that they might be willing for us parents to buy X, but if they were required to spend their money for it, they reevaluated their need or desire for the item. Now when they look at something at the store, I can see the wheels turning. They usually put it back, saying, 'I don't really need that.' My son even remarked, 'Mom, do you know how many times I'd have to mow the yard to pay for that?'"

There are many variations on our plan. Some parents give their older children enough money for their clothing budget and allow them to purchase their own clothes, staying within their budget. Others choose not to give an allowance at all but require their children to earn all of their money. Still others choose to give only an allowance and base the amount on the jobs the children do around the house. The important thing is that children know, before they are grown, how to handle money wisely and to keep a simple budget.

Precept upon Precept

Training children requires precept upon precept, line upon line. You must teach over and over, whether you are teaching good habits, academics, or spiritual concepts.

Whoever is faithful in very little is also faithful in much.

—Luke 16:10

Can you envision your child at the end of your training? One friend of mine makes a list of all the tasks she wants her children to learn and divides them loosely into age-appropriate categories. When a child has mastered all the tasks in the first level, he moves to the next level and helps his younger siblings with the tasks he has mastered and they are still learning. As the child encounters each new task, my friend carefully teaches how to do the task well and supervises until she is sure the child knows how to do the job correctly. By approximately age twelve, her children have mastered enough of the basic household tasks for them to manage the home, if necessary.

When you know where you are going, it isn't as difficult to get there. Once you can articulate what you want your children to learn, it's easier to teach them. Take small steps, teach the basics, do first things first, and deal with problems as they arise. Simple, right? I wish it were. Even so, the dream to have children who fulfill your heart's desire is possible: children who become well-balanced adults who love the Lord and other people and who will go out into the world to fulfill their particular calling from God and who, as adults, can function effectively to manage their homes and families and be of service to those around them.

Will we do it perfectly? No, we won't. I've never met parents who didn't wish they had done at least a few things differently. But the Lord knows you and each of your children intimately. He planned your particular family from the foundation of the world. He gave you the particular children you have for His purposes, and He doesn't make mistakes.

When you are distracted from the important things by all the necessary things, and you are searching for balance in your home, it may help to step back and view the bigger picture. One mom recounted to me how the Lord spoke to her on one occasion about what He had called her to do. Her husband was a firefighter who worked shifts, and she planned to accomplish a long list of chores before he got home at nine the next morning. Her seventeen-month-old daughter was already sleeping soundly that night, but her usually cooperative three-month-old son was awake to nurse again. As she recounted, "I was a bit frantic because I had not accomplished much on *my* list. I was nursing and rocking him in his bedroom and was so . . . well, stiff." She sang to him less than devotedly, but he just wouldn't sleep. "He cooed and smiled and 'gabbed.' It was very unlike him. He was awake and happy, and it was almost like he was trying to draw out of me the 'mommy' he knew and not this ice cube who just wanted him to go to sleep." Then she clearly sensed the Father saying to her, "It's not the *quantity* of things you do during the course of the day that make your day successful; it's the *quality* in which you do the things I've called you to do that make it a good day. Now, rock your baby. Rock him and enjoy him." My friend wept and rocked her baby. That night still reminds her to reevaluate any time her list becomes more important than the things the Lord has put before her at that moment.

All parents have received the gift of unconditional love from their children. It is our responsibility to train them and love them as we hold and cherish our most precious possession. Our labor of love is God's way of reminding us that He loves us unconditionally as He trains us.

Stop, Look, Think

Direction—Where Are You Going?

1. Go back to chapter 2 and recall your areas of struggle with skills. Which of these are having the most adverse effect on your children right now? Begin training your children in those areas first as you work to improve.

2. Take time to observe your children closely to discern their current weaknesses and strengths in various skill areas.

3. Record those strengths and weaknesses on the chart found on the accompanying CD (Weakness/Strength Evaluation) or simply make a list of each child's weaknesses and strengths. If you use the chart, record each child's name in a slot and put a W (weakness) or S (strength) in the box in the corresponding row. If neither applies, leave the box blank. Add to the chart any additional weaknesses and strengths you see in your children. This record is not for display. It is for your use as you pray for and train each child.

4. Make a list of simple, enforceable rules your family needs to follow and post them on the refrigerator, bulletin board, or other place for all family members to see. Assign individual chores that will help children work on their particular weaknesses and bring out particular strengths.

5. If you do not have a system to assign household chores to your children, devise one or find a method you can implement consistently. See sample forms on the CD.

6. If needed, plan a time for a clean-out day for your children's rooms. Follow through until each room is cleaned and straightened.

Devotion—What Are You Thinking?

1. Read 1 Thessalonians 5:18 and Ephesians 6:4. Is your attitude toward your home and the dailiness of life a good example to your children? Confess to the Lord any sin in your attitude and ask Him to forgive you and change your heart.

2. Are you training your children with kindness and patience? Read these verses and recall them when you are impatient and tired: Isaiah 40:28–31. Memorize Isaiah 40:29. Record the verses on a card and post them where you can see them and recall them when you need immediate encouragement.

3. Confess to the Lord the frustrations you have in teaching your children life skills. Ask Him to direct your plans to improve your training methods (see Proverbs 22:6).

Notes

Chapter 5
Paper by the Pile

I have a philosophy about paper. Paper is similar to meal leftovers—a bit here and a bit there until you've accumulated lots of pieces pushed aside like those small tidbits of food in the back of the refrigerator. Soon they're no longer useful because they expired; they are no longer of interest; they are replaced because you couldn't find the original; or they are worthless to you in other ways. In fact, a food leftover could be more useful than those paper bits since your students could at least use the moldy food for a science experiment!

Controlling paper is one of our biggest household challenges. I never realized the quantity of paper that could come into my home until I began to home teach. Certainly I can testify that the advent of the computer has not cut my paper volume or moved me closer to a paperless existence! We live in a world of information overload, and we mirror that with the volume of paper that invades our lives.

When we add curriculum catalogs, homeschooling publications, support group newsletters, children's schoolwork and artwork, and school record-keeping to our normal surplus of junk mail and papers, the flood can be relentless. Unless we control it, it will control us.

Under the Pile

Paper clutter overtakes you for the same reasons that other clutter accumulates. If you are visually oriented, you like to *see* your paper and possessions because they remind you of what you need to do. The problem is that the piles keep you from seeing everything you need to see and you forget what is under the pile. Use paper storage that allows you to see your items or close them away, whichever is more comfortable for you.

Another reason paper and things clutter your space is that you haven't designated a place to store them. I can demonstrate this *law of place* with a simple illustration: You have a lovely living room with a nice silk-flower arrangement in the center of the coffee table. If you're the mother of a toddler, just pretend! A friend visits to show you her new curriculum, and the two of you sit in the living room drinking tea, talking, and looking at the materials. The children are sitting quietly—remember, we're pretending—at the dining table with refreshments to keep them occupied. You move the flower arrangement to make room for the tea and the books. When you're finished and your friend leaves, what do you automatically do? Put the flower arrangement back in the center of the coffee table, right? You had mentally assigned it a place and you automatically returned it there when you were finished. The more you assign convenient places for your paper and other things, the less you will pile those things.

Two additional reasons paper clutter sneaks up on you are the same reasons I discussed in the clutter chapter: not storing things near where you most frequently use them, making it inconvenient to put them away, and difficulty making decisions about your possessions. These reasons apply equally to paper piles.

If you are under the pile, you may never have acquired control of your paper, thus the pile; or you may have cleaned out but didn't maintain, thus new piles. Digging out from under the pile is one challenge; controlling and maintaining paper flow is another. The latter is much easier.

Ill habits gather by unseen degrees—
As brooks make rivers,
rivers run to seas.

—John Dryden, *Little Things*

Types of Paper

Recognizing the types of paper in your life can help you evaluate how to deal with them, making it easier to realistically handle and maintain them. Too often some of us view paper as one big category and are overwhelmed. Then the piles just build higher. I've never seen a scientific study on the percentage of obsolete or junk paper in people's lives, but judging from my own mail and piles to sort, I would guesstimate that most of us could trash 80 percent of the "paper weight" we own and shuffle. Years ago, when my children and I took a field trip to a newspaper publishing company and saw the huge bundles of paper ready to run through the printing presses, I thought about how large a pile there would be in my home if I stacked all my paper. The image made me shudder!

As I examined my paper, I saw the following types:

- Bills
- Important financial papers and records
- School (mom and student papers) and other children's papers—some to keep and some to toss (see chapter 6)
- Papers to read (newsletters, magazines, articles, and so forth)—some to keep and some to toss
- Papers to give to others (support group, meetings, and so forth)
- Papers that require a response (an order, a phone call to make)
- Last (and certainly not least in quantity)—junk mail

Paper Questions

As you sort and maintain paper, answer three questions to help you know what to keep.

1. *What do I really need?* Determine if the paper is irreplaceable or vital to your life.
2. *Why do I need it?* How much paper do you keep just because it came into your life? Answer why you need that particular piece of paper.
3. *Who else needs it?* Some of the paper in your life is there because others need it now or in the future. For example, keep such records as financial and health insurance papers and papers that authenticate student work.

When you answer these questions, paper is less complicated to sort and store for easy retrieval.

Paper Guidelines

Many of the principles about clutter that you learned in chapter 3 apply to taming paper clutter as well: seek simplicity, identify junk, apply the happy mess test, start small, and use containers. Use those principles, or your version of them, to dig out from under the piles. However, paper demands at least the following five additional guidelines:

Retrieve It

If you aren't able to retrieve paper, it is of no value to you. The stress level of searching continually for a needed paper is too high a price to pay. You will love it when your paper is retrievable in just a moment. Find a simple system for retrieval and filing that works for you (keep reading).

Productivity in the eyes of the world is
not God's standard for organization.

—Terry Dorian, *Anyone Can Homeschool*

Deal with Mail

Mail is the single most troublesome paper we handle. Open mail daily, sitting or standing by the trash can, paper shredder, or paper recycling bin. I have permission from my husband to open any obvious junk mail addressed to him, examine it, and toss any irrelevant items. A paper shredder is an inexpensive security investment. When you receive anything in an envelope, keep the envelope only if you need to prove a postmark date. You have one less piece of paper if you toss it.

If you simply cannot examine the mail when it arrives or your spouse is the official mail opener in your house, use a container—a pretty basket or box—in a convenient place until someone opens the mail later in the day. A designated container looks nicer than a stack of paper and mail on the kitchen counter or other surface. Keep reading for more about what to do with the useful mail after you open it.

Create a Central Center for Paper

You can better control paper by keeping it in one place. Create a work center in your home to keep most of your paper: a desk, a cabinet, or even a closet converted into a work area so you can close the door. Wherever you choose, herd as much paper as possible to that place. If you have a phone and calendar available there as well, you can do most paper chores from that spot.

File It. Don't Pile It!

Have you noticed how the piles get higher when you don't deal with them? The paper fairy never comes, and your piles are still there the next morning. The quicker you deal with paper the less digging out you will have to do. See chapter 6 for file system ideas.

Control Paper

Control of incoming mail and other paper, including paper you and your children produce, is essential to staying on top of paper clutter. You are not obligated to keep or store a paper just because it comes into your life. In fact, if paper is a struggle for you, be cautious about ways you produce or receive more paper. I try not to accept business cards or information if the person can e-mail me instead. This strategy isn't always possible, of course; but when it is, I have less paper in my home.

Do you really need a five-year-old curriculum catalog? If the company is still in business, personnel will gladly send you a current one or you can obtain one online. If you receive a catalog that you won't order from this year but you may in the future, tear out and file relevant pages as well as the contact page to obtain a new one later. You don't have to store the entire catalog. To cut down on paper volume make deliberate choices about what to keep and what you can replace later.

Most of us tend to put magazines on equal footing with books. We hate to throw them away. However, articles in magazines are outdated quickly, and the content is full of advertising that is certainly outdated. With the advent of the Internet, it is possible to search for information on any topic imaginable, which makes it even less desirable to save boxes and boxes of old magazines. My favorite magazine has an online archive that goes back to 1996, and I can find almost anything of interest. Unless you have filed and categorized your magazines making it possible to go back to any article that you are looking for, the boxes do you no good—remember the retrievable factor! If you have a favorite article that you must save, tear it from the magazine and file it, including the magazine title and issue date. Books and magazines are among the heaviest items that people haul with them when they move. If you have not read a magazine in the last six months, the odds of your doing so are very slim. Either share it with someone else who may be interested or toss it!

F SHARP Paper Routing System

Years ago I read that you should only touch paper once and deal with it as soon as you handle it. Obviously, the author of this bit of organizational insight didn't have a houseful of children, lessons to teach, and floors to mop!

You see, most moms' problem is a continuous flow of paper that demands attention but a limited time to deal with it. What should you do with the screaming pieces of paper until you can take a few minutes to focus on them? If you put them on your desk or the kitchen counter, they disappear under the pile and you promptly forget them. You need to route the paper to a retrievable place until you can take time to manage it. Perhaps this simple F SHARP Paper Routing System will help you.

The acronym F SHARP reminds you of the actions to take with paper until you permanently store or discard it:

F—File It
S—Send It
H—Hold It
A—Answer It
R—Read It
P—Pay It

Before we look at each category, the first thing to note is that this is a temporary routing system. You still must deal with the paper, but you can locate it and take the needed action at a time that is convenient for you. This isn't a crutch so you can ignore the paper in your life; the piles will pile, even in this system, if you don't maintain and take proper action with your paper flow. However, F SHARP contains the paper for easy retrieval. Let's look at each category.

F—File It

These necessary papers are the ones you must file or store. Put important financial papers, items for homeschooling, medical records, and anything that you should save into a *shallow* file tray or box, waiting until you can take fifteen minutes to file them in your file system. See chapter 6 for help with categories for filing. You should seize a moment here and there to keep your tray empty or low—the reason for the shallow tray! If you do not allow the tray to overflow, you can file all you have added to it in just a few minutes. Filing immediately is best, but your File It tray holds the things that must wait.

S—Send It

The items you need to send or give to someone outside your home should go into a folder or basket or both. In a folder you might put pictures to mail to relatives, papers to take to church or your support group meeting, copies to make at an outside copy store, or documents you need to take with you when you leave your house. Library books and three-dimensional items could go in a large basket or container beside the door in which you enter and leave. Encourage your children to add their completed library books to the basket so you aren't scrambling around the house searching for them when it's time to return them. Anything that must leave your home can go into a folder or back-door container so it is available when you walk out the door.

H—Hold It

Have you ever placed an order for school materials only to lose the order form before the items arrived? Possibly you have noticed an error on an invoice that the company needed to correct, and you are waiting for an answer from the accounting department. Where do you put the bill while the credit is processing? Add anything that needs further attention to the Hold It file. You will know exactly where to find the pending paper when you have to give it attention again. Once you settle the issue, file the paper, put it in File It until a later file session, or discard it.

A—Answer It

This category differs from Hold It, although one mother told me she combined the two for a simple Action folder. Answer It contains items that need your response when you receive them—an inquiry, a business or personal letter to answer, a note to yourself to make a particular phone call—anything that requires action on your part. You might move an item from this folder to the Hold It file if you have done what you need to do and are waiting for an answer in return.

R—Read It

Make a file folder for small items you need to read: support-group newsletters, church announcements, brochures, your child's latest essay, and so forth. Additionally, place a basket or container beside your favorite chair for your substantive reading material or the current family read-aloud book. Keep this container cleaned out about every three or four months. If you haven't read something in the basket for that long, you probably won't.

P—Pay It

You and your spouse may already have a system for keeping up with your bills. If so, you may not need this category. Many people keep track of their bills on the computer, but they often need a place to put paper bills as well. If you do not have a bill system and you are plagued with lost bills that you fail to pay on time, this folder can be a money-saver. When a bill arrives, open it and circle or write the due date with a black or red marker. Put the bill into your Pay It folder so you can find it when it is bill-paying time. For quick reference you might note on the outside of the folder the dates that recurring items are due and place the bills in the folder in the order of the due dates.

Personalizing the System

Don't put the folders for the various categories away in a file cabinet or closed container. Instead, put them in a wire stand-up file holder on your desk or in your Central Center near the File It tray. Having easy access is the key to using them. If you like color, use a different color folder for each category: green for Send It, red for Hold It, yellow for Answer It, blue for Read It, and purple for Pay It. These are merely suggestions, so use any other colors you choose.

If you have special circumstances, you may want to add other categories and folders. However, don't complicate your F SHARP system. If it is simple, you will more likely use it and see the piles disappear.

The following suggestions may be helpful for any special circumstance in your life.

An Action or Hot folder is helpful to separate urgent things for attention. That's the first folder you choose when you make time to deal with your paper.

If you are involved in leadership or activities that require frequent phone calls, you may want a special folder labeled Calls where you put items that require telephone time.

My husband's job required frequent travel for a number of years, so I kept a folder with his name on it for anything that I saved for him or for reminders for me to tell him something important. If you have older children or teens, you may want a folder for each family member for mail or notes to them.

A folder labeled Coupons to Clip could hold the sheets of coupons that come in the mail or newspaper until you have your children cut them out for you— a great job for kids!

Your may need a folder for any special interests in order to keep those items apart from other files. For example, I keep a folder in my wire rack for a church ministry that my husband and I supervise. It needs to be handy for quick reference since I use it frequently.

If you want to make better use of your wait time at doctors' or dentists' offices or children's lessons and practices, you could keep a folder labeled Paper Wait to work on during those often-wasted segments of time spent waiting. Be sure to put it in your Send It basket by the door to pick up as you leave.

Use any category that helps you handle particular papers, but limit the number of folders you use. My personal system has only one additional folder added to the F SHARP categories. F SHARP isn't your file system; it is a paper routing system to help you retrieve your papers when you need to file them, use them, or discard them.

Consistency and Persistence

Remember that F SHARP is a *temporary* paper routing system. If you have a huge mountain of papers, begin this routing system to cut off the flow and gain control while you gradually handle the accumulated pile. Set a goal of ten or fifteen minutes a day to deal with the paper that continues to stream into your home. That few minutes will save you hours in the future. If a few minutes a day is sufficient to handle your volume of paper, you are doing well. If not, add a longer time at least once a week to work on paper. The investment of time will bring peace of mind and order to your life. Treat the mountain of paper just as you would any other clutter clean-out, using the clutter principles you learned in chapter 3.

Don't worry about anything, but in everything, through prayer and petition with thanksgiving, let your requests be made known to God. And the peace of God, which surpasses every thought, will guard your hearts and your minds in Christ Jesus.

—*Philippians 4:6–7*

Sisyphus, a Greek mythological character, faced eternal punishment for his sins with a task of hard labor. He was required to roll a giant boulder to the top of a hill. With great effort and toil, he pushed and shoved until he reached the top at the end of the day, only to have the boulder roll back down the hill. His labor began again each day. At times, we feel that our paper clutter battle is like Sisyphus' chore, endless and discouraging.

Don't give up! You may not defeat your paper clutter overnight. Nevertheless, you can make progress if you have a plan, and the Lord will give you success if you're willing. Take one step at a time, gain control of incoming paper, and gradually deal with your accumulated papers.

After you work through the chapter exercises below, let's look at some options for record-keeping and a file system.

 ## Stop, Look, Think

 ## Direction—Where Are You Going?

1. If you are under a paper pile, determine the reason(s). Are you using improper storage for your paper? Have you determined a good place for it? Is it inconvenient to put away? Do you have difficulty making decisions about what to do with it? What do you need to change?

2. Do you need a simple revival of your paper system, using any of the ideas in this chapter or others of your own, or do you have stacks and stacks of paper to deal with? Determine a plan for sorting your paper based on the degree to which you need improvement. Use the clutter principles you learned in chapter 3 and the paper guidelines in this chapter to improve your current system or lack of one.

3. Do you have a current method of dealing with paper flow and incoming paper? If not, try the F SHARP system to see if it helps you. If it doesn't serve your purpose, find another way to quickly deal with paper until you can take time to attend to it.

Devotion—What Are You Thinking?

1. How is the paper in your life affecting you emotionally and spiritually? Are there sins you need to confess to the Lord concerning discipline with paper?

2. Read Proverbs 16:3 and Philippians 4:19. Know that your efforts to bring paper under control will bring honor to the Lord in your home.

3. Ask the Lord for guidance and for diligence in handling paper. Check back on your progress and continue to place your efforts before the Lord.

Notes

Chapter 6
Record-keeping Made Easy

I have a confession to make; I dislike filling out forms! This admission wouldn't be so extraordinary except that I've designed dozens and dozens of forms for homeschoolers (*The Time Minder*, Rockett, 1987–1993, out of print; and *The Home School Manual*, 5th, 6th, and 7th editions, Theodore Wade, Jr. & Others, Gazelle Publications, 1993–1998, appendix of record-keeping forms).

Although there are as many different ways to put lines on paper to make a form as there are people who create them, many forms are too complicated to use because they are not generic enough to apply to various situations. What's more, blank spaces on a form seem to insist—no, demand—that I fill them out, even when I don't know what to write there.

Record-keeping can be a great frustration for homeschool families. Even if you have no external agent such as oversight programs, state requirements, and so forth dictating a particular set of recorded information about your children's schooling, common sense says that it is wise to keep track of a few things. Which records do you need? How bound by record-keeping should you be? Your head will soon spin when you add to those questions others about homeschooling—methods, student learning styles, and mom's teaching styles—that may necessitate different approaches to record-keeping.

If you have a background in classroom teaching, you may view record-keeping in a way different from someone who uses an unschooling or relaxed homeschooling method. Additionally, one of your children may need one learning approach and type of record, while another one needs entirely different approaches and record-keeping. A look at the big picture will make it easier to sort out why and how to use planning and records for your benefit.

The Big Picture

Let's examine the important overall view of record-keeping—creating and using records—before tackling specific record-keeping methods and forms.

Your family is not a school, and you have no need to duplicate one. You're a family, made up of parent(s) and child(ren), not an institution of administrators and students. You have relationships that enlighten you about your children's needs, but administrators either don't know students' individual needs or have to discern them mostly through means of records. You have freedom in homeschooling to do anything that meets your goals of raising and educating your children, and likely you will have different reasons for using records than an institution would have. You also are able to change your record-keeping methods whenever they aren't meeting yours or your children's needs, something that a bureaucracy either can't do at all or accomplishes only with great difficulty.

There is not just one way to keep records. Even as your family priorities must fit your family and may differ from other families' priorities, your record-keeping methods should reflect your personal style and not mimic others' methods if their methods don't suit you and your family. The younger your children are the less formal school record-keeping you need. A simple journal may suffice for keeping track of needed information at those young ages.

A good plan today is better than a perfect plan tomorrow.

—A Proverb, *http://en.thinkexist.com*

Forms and plan books are your tools and, used wisely, free you for the more important tasks of living and learning. It's probably a safe assumption that you don't have the luxury of time for everything you would like to do. However, you need *some* reasonable planning and record-keeping to manage your home well and teach your children without trapping yourself in a cycle of frustration and lack of accomplishment. Good planning does take time but not as much as you might think. Take a few minutes a day or a longer time weekly to plan. A small investment of time and attention in your personalized method pays big dividends.

Conversely, excessive rigidity is the antithesis to little or no planning. If you overplan and lack flexibility, you will make yourself and your family miserable and accomplish little beyond filling out forms. Begin with a base plan and expand as your circumstance requires, but if you try to micromanage too many details, you will defeat yourself. Your starting place is a general plan for home and school that you can add to if the need arises.

Ask yourself if the tools you have chosen to use are enabling you to accomplish the necessary and important tasks. If not, consider whether the particular tool is the cause of the failure, requiring you to try something else, or if you are diligently using it for the best result.

A Plan to Plan

How can you sort out which home and school planning and record-keeping tools you may need? Let's take the process in parts as we plan to plan.

Decide

Consider the questions we examined in chapter 5 that helped you sort paper clutter. *What do I need? Why do I need it? Who else needs it?* These same questions apply to discerning which forms and tools you need for your household and for school records. Choose forms or methods of record-keeping that allow you to gather needed information, which is the form's purpose, and eliminate unnecessary forms or portions of forms that you don't need. Your individual situation determines how many details you need. If you need all-inclusive permission to leave any portion of a form blank that isn't necessary, you now have it!

> By failing to prepare you are
> preparing to fail.
>
> —Benjamin Franklin, *www.wisdomquotes.com*

Your record-keeping style, the ages and number of children in your family, your available time, and your state homeschool requirements for school records are among the factors to consider as you decide which record-keeping tools will benefit you. Freely experiment with forms and ways to keep the records that fit your situation. Know clearly the purpose for recording the particular information on a form. If you don't need that information, don't waste your precious time using that form or portion of a form.

Apply the rule "first need—future need" when you consider using a specific form. Do you need the information now for evaluating and planning home and school? Will you need the information in the future for reporting, evaluating, encouraging, or for changes in your schooling situation?

Available on the CD are numerous forms for home and school. A master list of descriptions and instructions is included on the CD (File-a-Plan Forms List: Descriptions and Instructions), and a list of brief form descriptions is in Appendix D to help you choose any that could benefit you. Choose from these forms, purchase other forms, continue to use forms or planners you already use, or create your own by hand or on computer. Use only the ones you are comfortable using and that help you manage your home and school.

For household planning needs, begin with the suggestions in the previous chapters for establishing priorities, setting goals, evaluating your household, tracking your to-do's and projects, and establishing chore assignments for children. Additional household forms on the CD, including a generic meal plan sheet, might be helpful for you.

Regardless of your situation or learning method, use a few basic record-keeping tools for yourself and for your children's requirements. Each child is an individual with individual needs. You may use more structure with one and less with another. My focus in this book isn't on learning styles and methods; others have written effectively about those issues (see Resources in Appendix A). No matter which method or philosophy you use in schooling, set goals so you know where you're going. You might use a school mission statement to direct your school year and a goal sheet to help your student arrive there.

Don't worry about such institutional terms as "Course of Study" or "Scope and Sequence" for planning. Simply lay out the material you plan to use for the year on the Study Plan form found on the CD. This sheet allows you to record in one place your student's subject areas, including unit studies, curriculum, their sources for ordering purposes, and your notes. You don't have to be overly concerned about having this sheet complete for the entire year. If you make changes, you can add those later. An additional Subject or Unit Worksheet gives a bit more detail for study planning.

> # Plans fail when there is no counsel, but with many advisers they succeed.
>
> *—Proverbs 15:22*

Other basic records could include a way to record schoolwork done by the student, filled out by you or the student before or after the student does the work; a transcript or portfolio for older students; and anything else that applies to your special circumstances or that you want to track. Since you have numerous choices on the CD, choose the ones that help you and your students reach your goals.

Divide

It is easy to feel overwhelmed when we view the entire picture of our responsibilities. Breaking down home and school responsibilities into bite-size pieces by effective planning keeps you on track and helps establish balance in your life. Feel free to experiment with various forms and abandon any that don't seem to work for you. *Do not* feel compelled to use any forms that do not accomplish that greater purpose.

All organization systems have one factor in common: they break down an ultimate goal into smaller goals that are reachable on a daily basis.

—Mary Ann Froehlich, *What's a Smart Woman Doing In a Place Like This?*

Do look at the big picture and see how you can divide it into smaller plans. For example, if you plot a basic schedule that is applicable for your week on the Master Household Routine, you can then break your day into specifics with chore and school assignments by using the Daily Works sheet or Weekly Works sheet.

For school you might begin with the Subject or Unit Worksheet for each study area and then use the Weekly Studies Log to show how you are implementing those goals daily. When you view an academic goal, determine how you will break that goal into pieces so that you accomplish the goal by the end of the year or by the end of a general time period. Any big task is only as large as the next step; learn to divide and conquer, using any tools that help you do that.

Document

For each student keep an academic portfolio that contains a record of completed schoolwork, samples of work, important information about the student, special activities, and any other information you feel is necessary. Even if you live in a state that does not require that data, you will find it useful when you evaluate your student's progress by looking at past years and comparing them to the present one.

When your student is young, it might be beneficial for you to start a list of *every* activity in which he participates, from sports to church to charity volunteer work to music or other lessons, and so forth. Keep a high school transcript for high school students. There is no particular form you *must* use, but you may like the one included on the CD since it is specific to homeschoolers.

Whether you choose forms to help you plan or choose to use none at all and merely record notes in a notebook, keep your plan simple and uncomplicated. Your records are the means and not the end.

Setting Up Files

Once you've chosen which records you will keep and how you will keep them, you still have to store those records for reference. While in theory the computer should cut the volume of paper records you have to store, there are still items that are difficult to keep on a computer. Without a planned way to file your records, you will end up with more paper clutter.

You may already own a filing cabinet where you store current records. A file cabinet is nice to have, but don't be restricted by the normal two- or four-drawer traditional file system. Smaller filing containers are less expensive and take up less space than a large file cabinet. File boxes or crates, desktop sorters, or portable file containers are useful for your current school year records; keep school records in one container and home records in another; or if you have older students, you can use separate file containers for the students so that they can learn to maintain their own records. If your containers are portable, you can store them in your Central Center (chapter 5) and transport them where you need them.

You can keep daily school records in a notebook for all students or in folders—one for each student—and keep the notebook or folders in an open storage on a desk or in your Central Center. If you are a right-brain-dominant person who likes to see files and folders, use a wire divider on your desk for your most used files, or use a cubbyhole container on your desk in which to keep current files. Only use a closed vertical-type file container for files you need to store.

A complicated, detailed file system may be necessary for an office, but it may not be the most functional for home. Think in larger categories rather than filing under every possible category. You can locate things more easily when you use fewer groupings. A good test for determining if you need a new category is to ask two questions:

Will I have at least five to ten papers in that folder?

Will I need to use a folder for each student in that category?

If you can answer in the affirmative to either question, add the category.

File-a-Plan

You are the only one who can determine which file categories you need for your home and school. Appendix B (File-a-Plan Category List) is a list of possible categories and the forms and papers you would file in each category. Scan the list to choose which might be applicable for you. No one will use every category on the list. An asterisk (*) by the category name indicates applicable forms provided on the CD for that category. The CD includes the forms and descriptions with instructions for use.

When you know which records you want to keep and in what container you will file/store them, you're ready to set up folders for your files. Use hanging file folders where possible, labeled alphabetically with the categories you intend to use. If you love color, you might use one color file folder for household files and one for school files, or you may choose to use a different color for each child's folders for quick distinction. When you set up your files, it will be easy to file items quickly and combat paper clutter.

Decisions about where to file particular papers are often confusing. Two reference guides included on the CD may assist you: The File-a-Plan Category Reference sheets and the Easy Guide Index.

Print only the Category Reference sheets that match the categories you use in your file, and file each at the front of the hanging file folder that matches the category. For example, if you use a Field Trips category, you would print the Field Trips sheet and file it in front of any folders you file in the Field Trips hanging file folder. This sheet guides you in what to file in that category and what and when to archive paper in that folder. See more detailed instructions on the CD.

If you print the Easy Guide Index, create a hanging file folder labeled Easy Guide Index at the front of all your other folders and file the Index in that folder for easy access. For quick reference, you might include in the Easy Guide Index folder a printed copy of the File-a-Plan Category List (different from the Category Reference sheets) and the File-a-Plan Forms List: Descriptions and Instructions and the File-a-Plan Archive Category List.

Archive

In time every file container fills to capacity and crowds your needed records with those you should shift to another location or those you no longer need. A once-a-year clean-out is necessary to control the volume of useless papers in your files. A one-year warranty that has been in your files for five years is worthless, especially if you no longer own the item.

The File-a-Plan Archive can help make your files more functional and is just as much a part of your filing system as the active files. Even if you decide not to use any of the suggestions in this book for your filing and paper control, I encourage you to make your own archive and use it regularly.

The Archive is a place for records you don't use frequently but may need in the future. Use a separate drawer in a file cabinet or use a different, smaller file container for your Archive to keep it out of the way of your current active files and papers. However, keep it in an accessible place, or you will be tempted not to use it.

See Appendix C (File-a-Plan Archive Category List) for a suggested list of possible categories for your archives. Choose the ones that will help you and ignore the ones you don't need.

One of the most useful parts of the File-a-Plan System is the Category Reference sheets, and they are especially helpful when you are ready to archive papers. If you have printed a sheet for each category contained in your active files, simply preview the information on the sheet for any category and judge when to remove material and where to put it. As you use active files, you will learn which documents are important to retain.

The Category Reference sheets and the Easy Guide Index make it easy for others to use your files and consistently file papers in the correct places. Perhaps an older child can file, and you may never have to do it again! Think what wonderful training it will be for your children.

Forms, Files, and a Final Word

Some of you reading this chapter will be anxious to set up files or improve the ones you have. The entire idea of filling out forms and keeping neat, accurate records appeals to you, and you find that forms and records help you do a better job teaching your children. That's great! I encourage you to use anything available to help you along the way. However, I remind you that the records are a means to an end and not the end itself. Your family should remain central. You are not a teacher or an administrator in an institutional school; you are a mom! Be the best at that job you can be and your children will learn.

> Let me encourage you to look up from time to time and remind yourself of your goals. Goals may be simple or elaborate, but they are our focal point. Goals are the place toward which we aim.
>
> —Debbie Strayer, *Gaining Confidence to Teach*

Conversely, if you hate to fill out forms, as I do, but you know you should keep *some* records, even for your own benefit, I encourage you to keep it simple and persevere. Make the records and files work for you rather than becoming a slave to a system. The point is to use the records as your aid to stay on track and do a better job teaching your children. You are a mom, and you don't have to make your records look as though they belong in a school.

No matter whether you fall into the love-forms or the hate-forms group, you have the same challenges. Set goals—no matter how you record them. Constantly assess your progress—with or without forms. Be a student of each of your children; they are individuals. Pray and trust God to guide you; He gave you these particular children. If you are able to identify and discard *school-type* ideas of education, no matter how you decide to keep records, you and your children will benefit as you learn and grow together. The memories you gather will be the most important record you keep.

Stop, Look, Think

Direction—Where Are You Going?

1. Have you become too lax in your record-keeping or too rigid in keeping your schedule? Where do you need to change your goals and expectations?
2. Using the principles from this chapter, improve your current record-keeping or start a simple record-keeping system with the basics of needed information. Choose forms or tools that you need to add and eliminate forms that you discover you don't really need.
3. Do you have an archive established for your records? If not, set it up and clean out your files.

Devotion—What Are You Thinking?

1. Has *school* swallowed up your family? Have you forgotten why you are educating your children at home? If so, confess it to the Lord and ask Him to show you the balance for your household.
2. Remember that God keeps records—those of the generations (Matthew 1:1 is one example), the Ten Commandments on tablets of stone, and names in the Book of Life (Revelation 20:11–12; 21:27). He also asks man to keep records—the Bible, divinely inspired and written by man, records God's revelation to us. He told others to write or record information that He wants man to remember. ("Write down this vision;

clearly inscribe it on tablets so one may easily read it" (Habakkuk 2:2). Use a concordance to find Scriptures that contain the words *write* and *record*. Write one or two of these in a place where you keep your records to remind you that you have a purpose for keeping your records.

Are you interested in a printed and boxed kit of the File-a-Plan System? If produced, it would be ready to use by simply opening the box, placing dividers into your own hanging file folders, and choosing and preparing your individualized file folders in categories that are useful to you. If such a product interests you, please contact the author, Marilyn Rockett, at Marilyn@MarilynRockett.com to let her know.

Marilyn also welcomes your thoughts on this book.

Notes

Chapter 7
Real Life around the House

After teaching my sons for fifteen years, I'm convinced that homeschooling is the hardest easy thing I've ever done. I'm in good company since most families make homeschooling too complicated. I did at times. It doesn't have to be complicated or difficult, but it does need to be thoughtfully intentional. Homeschoolers read all the proper books and idealize how their home and school should look; sometimes they frustrate themselves because real life—that remarkable mixture of the mundane and the unsuspected—happens every day and not necessarily by the book. Parents can sometimes be more the problem than their homeschool effort.

Ruth Beechick, author of *You Can Teach Your Child Successfully*, says, "If you find yourself struggling to mold your child to a book, try reversing priorities. It's the child you are teaching, not the book."[1] You can apply this wisdom to your household as well. If you find yourself struggling to mold your family to your school, you should try reversing priorities. It's the family you are dealing with, not the school.

The speed of life often calls for special measures to help you maintain and accomplish the things that seem to pile up around you. Homeschooling affords the opportunity for you to jump off the daily merry-go-round and take inventory when your plans don't seem to be going well or when the Lord brings unexpected events into your life. You are able to fit school around the family. Teacher workshop days provide teachers with better preparation for their jobs; feel free to set aside similar times but do it on *your* schedule.

Special Challenges

It is impossible in this book's scope to address every unusual circumstance that may arise in homeschool families. Authors have written extensively about homeschooling special-needs children and the accompanying demands, getting organized while using a specific homeschool method, beginning to homeschool, keeping structured or relaxed records, blending family with education, teaching older children while handling toddlers, single-parent homeschooling, and so forth. Many families juggle challenges of home teaching while traveling, caring for grandparents in the home, adjusting their schedules around Dad's unusual work demands, homeschooling through a major family illness or accident, and many more circumstances.

Let us view our organization systems as tools to help our families, not see our families as enemies of our organization systems.

—Mary Ann Froehlich, *What's a Smart Woman Like You Doing In a Place Like This?*

Wonderful resources are available, and I encourage you to use any that are helpful to you. Even if life is going smoothly now, you will eventually come face-to-face with real-life challenges where your well-laid plans seem to evaporate as fast as your children disappear at chore time.

Real-life Lessons

When real-life difficulties happen, use them to your advantage. Temporarily scrap the curriculum and most of the schedule and deal with your circumstance. It is a God-ordained time of learning and living for your family, and you may learn more important lessons than those in the books.

Our family experienced one of those life-learning lessons when we began to homeschool. The Lord customized the situation just for me because in the beginning I was afraid to abandon school for fear I wouldn't do an adequate job teaching my boys if I didn't exactly follow the plan.

Our second son, then eleven years old, had a difficult time doing well in a classroom setting although he tested quite well in every area. We had taken him out of the sixth grade to homeschool him. Since he was young for his grade, our rationale was that if he didn't do well at home—meaning if I didn't do well teaching him—we could always put him back in school the next year to repeat the same grade. In that case he would be in the grade that he probably should have been in all along, and he would benefit from that.

Thus, I set out with all my plans and schedules and good intentions to do the best job I could do teaching my son. In God's plans we also started building a new house that year, contracting it ourselves. My husband's job required frequent out-of-town travel during that time, and I often had to meet a plumber, electrician, or other subcontractor at the house with instructions for the job. I recall tears and moans to my husband, saying that I would never be able to teach our son if I constantly had to stop what we were doing to run to the construction site a few miles away.

Since it cost us more in interim financing the longer we took to build the house, we were pushing our schedule. In November, with only two months of formal schooling under our belt, I threw my hands up and quit. I gave my son piles of classic books to read—he certainly hadn't gotten that good reading material in school—and we did an occasional math lesson. When we needed to go to the house site, our three youngest boys, which included two preschoolers, went along and helped any way they were able—picking up trash, measuring, hammering, and generally learning about building a house. We finished in late April and moved in, with the school year all but gone.

There is no cookie-cutter method for teaching and learning, not in a homeschool anyway.

—Paul and Gena Suarez, *Homeschooling Methods*

That was in the early '80s when the few homeschoolers in our area were hiding from school districts. I tearfully decided that if the school system ever found out how little real teaching I had done, they would put me *under* the jail and throw away the key. Yes, I actually used that cliché, and I laugh about it now. A local Christian school was protecting homeschoolers by administering standardized tests and keeping records on file. That enabled us to say that our children were under their supervision although they didn't provide materials or other helps. Our son had taken tests at the beginning of the school year, but when end-of-the-year testing time came, I was so frightened of the results that I couldn't sleep. The wait to get the test results back seemed endless, and I was sure that my short-lived homeschooling adventure was a failure.

The mail brought the test results, and I retrieved the tests from the beginning of the year before I opened the envelope. I laid the old and new results side by side and carefully compared the two. I was astounded! Our son had improved in every portion of the test—in some cases by two or three grade levels. How was that possible when we didn't do "school" and when *my* plans had failed? My theory is that our son was so relaxed after the pressure of continual failure in a classroom that he was truly learning at home from everything around him. I can't prove that theory, but homeschool statistics bear out that children learn best in a home environment with individual attention, even when it doesn't look much like institutional school.

My point is *not* that you only have to have your children read and do a little math for them to learn, nor am I suggesting that you be so relaxed that you don't have any goals or plans. You can't dump school indefinitely. My point is that life happens, and when special challenges arise, you and your family must adjust while still learning—the children *and* you.

I ran out of children just when I was getting the hang of homeschooling!

—Marilyn Rockett, *workshop seminars*

SOS Day

When you face challenging times that seem to divert you from your purpose and you need to reevaluate and regroup, you might try some unique ways to do that.

If your challenge is clutter that needs clearing and the only solution is to take a break from the normal routine to de-clutter, begin by declaring an SOS (Salvage Our Sanity) Day. If you're the mother of babies or toddlers, or if you simply are overwhelmed with clutter, you may need numerous SOS hours or even an SOS week or month. Nevertheless, it's possible to bring your house to order, piece by piece.

Giving your cleanout time a name such as SOS Day gives it an air of importance much like a teacher workshop day. It mentally moves the time to a priority and encourages you that real relief is ahead. You know that the clutter is temporary, tamable, and tolerable when you have a plan to deal with it. Plan this time in your schedule since cleaning out clutter is as important as any other household task you need to accomplish. It *does* save your sanity to win the battle with efficiency-robbing clutter. Decide on an hour, day, or week to give the clutter your attention and apply all that you learned in chapter 3 to bring order back to your life. You can then resume your normal schedule with more freedom, peace, and efficiency.

Ketchup Day

One way to regroup when you fall behind with normal tasks is to institute a Ketchup Day. I affectionately named it Ketchup (Catch Up) Day because, on those days, I planned a simple meal that often included ketchup. Like an SOS Day, it is a day to set aside the normal routine, at home and away from home, and be flexible. Your children won't be educational dunces because you use a day or two to catch up if you need it. In fact, they will probably appreciate a more relaxed mom because you catch up on some of the chores that call out to you for completion. Regardless of what you call it, home-teaching moms occasionally need a time like this to accomplish a few things that they have put off doing.

It's best if you intentionally and periodically plan a Ketchup Day, but at times you resort to one out of sheer desperation. Involve your children in any way that will help you or alternate childcare with a friend so each of you can have a Ketchup Day.

> The pace of life in our culture can be frantic. Homeschooling gives us the precious gift of time with our children.
>
> —Zan Tyler, *Anyone Can Homeschool*

In order to use your time most wisely, start a list of nonemergency tasks—the ones that you never seem to finish—in your notebook or planner or on the fourth column of your Running To-Do List (Nonemergency Tasks—chapter 2). If you prefer, make this list on a separate sheet of paper in order to post it where you can see it frequently. It could include such activities as tackling a stack of mending, cleaning the front porch or driveway, sorting through coupons, rearranging the bookshelf, planning a few guest meals, filing the stack of papers on your desk, and so forth. Add to this list as tasks arise and choose items from it on Ketchup Day.

Reserve Ketchup Day strictly for items from that list, resisting the temptation to do activities that day other than the minimum daily-routine tasks. Checking those worrisome items off your list will give you a sense of accomplishment, and you can resume your regular routine the following day. Ketchup Day is a time for you to catch up with your normal tasks and begin again—something every homeschool mother needs at times.

EDIT Day

Look for ways to incorporate a time in your schedule that will rebuild your energy and strength for your mothering mission. Plan an EDIT (Easy Does IT) Day occasionally. EDIT Day differs from an SOS Day or a Ketchup Day because of its focus: it's a time for mental, physical, and emotional recouping rather than for work. Your EDIT Day, or hour if that's all you can manage, can be a family day that is relaxing for you, a break to shop without children, a soak in a bubble bath with a book, a weekend retreat with your husband, or anything that helps you return to motherhood and home teaching with a renewed spirit.

Do you remember the last basic in chapter 2—take time for the Lord and for rest? Put it in your schedule! Your time with the Lord should be daily, of course, but rest time may come in packages other than daily. Don't wait until you're at the end of endurance. In this effort your husband can help most of all; he's your guardian, so communicate to him before you near the edge of the cliff. If you apply the principles you've learned about priorities and bringing your home to order, you will relax more in your everyday living, but even then, you need an occasional break.

Pay careful attention, then, to how you walk—not as unwise people but as wise—making the most of the time, because the days are evil.

—*Ephesians 5:15–16*

God's Plans

However you choose to manage your special circumstances, you have the freedom to use them for good for you and your family. When Hurricane Katrina hit the Gulf Coast and Rita slammed in right behind her in 2005, one homeschool friend and her family suspended their regular studies and joined the effort to help thousands of refugees that flooded into the Houston, Texas area. They gathered donations, cooked, baked, shuttled food to a nearby hotel full of refugees, helped people find what they needed while listening to them complain about what they were getting, and expanded their family of four in a small home to twelve. For weeks the children accomplished minimal progress in my friend's school planner, but they learned to be content with what they have, to care for strangers, and to minister the love of Jesus to the hurt and traumatized. As my friend said to me, "Obviously what God wanted us to learn far outweighed what I wanted the children to learn." You can't buy those kinds of lessons in a curriculum.

When you need to catch up, stop and benefit from flexibility rather than seeing obstacles as a diversion from what you really have to do. Your children can enjoy a change in routine, even if they are helping you on Ketchup Day or SOS Day. You are schooling when your children are learning real life around the house!

STOP Stop, Look, Think

Direction—Where Are You Going?

1. Have you been fitting the family around school rather than the other way around? Has your curriculum become paramount in your home? Determine if you are using methods that allow for *real life*. What do you need to change?
2. Start a Nonemergency Tasks list in your notebook, planner, or on other paper. Use the list when you have a Ketchup Day.

3. Do you need to plan an SOS Day or a Ketchup Day? Plan the day or time into your schedule now and decide what you will do during that special time—de-clutter or any other need from your list.

4. Have you had an EDIT Day lately? Ask your husband for help, if needed, and plan a refreshing outing soon.

Devotion—What Are You Thinking?

1. Do you trust the Lord when He brings real-life challenges into your home and family? If you struggle when circumstances change your plans, read Romans 8:24-30; Psalm 9:10; 28:7; 37:5; and Proverbs 3:5.

2. Confess to the Lord any area in which you do not trust Him. Ask Him to strengthen you and help you keep your eyes on Him.

3. Are you struggling with a special circumstance now? God is giving you a chance to lean on him and grow. Submit yourself to His plan and let your plans go.

Notes

Chapter 8
A Family—Not a School

May I ask you a question? Think before you answer, and answer honestly! If your children were in an institutional school and they left home every day, would your organization and household management habits really be any different than they are now? (long pause)

I ask that question because the temptation for most inundated homeschool moms is to blame the struggle on homeschooling or on the kids. "I could keep things more orderly if the kids were in school." "I have too much to do because I have eight children at home." "I can't stay ahead of the mess the kids make, and they're too young to help me." "I don't have time to do _____ because we have to finish lessons."

The problem with those responses is that they may not be completely true. Worse, they may lead us to forget why we're homeschooling and cause us to question the wisdom of continuing. Yes, we have our hands full, and I'm not treating that lightly. I've been there. Yes, it's hard work and a tough job to add lessons to our usual responsibilities. It's necessary to adjust our thinking about homekeeping duties to allow for the extra load. Yes, the children are home all day, and it seems that they create messes as quickly as we can clean them up.

The mother's heart is the child's schoolroom.

—Henry Ward Beecher, *http://en.thinkexist.com*

But isn't it also true that if our children were gone and we didn't teach them, we would still have just as many mouths to feed, just as much laundry to wash, just as many children who need help with homework, and just as many to train— and less time with them to accomplish it? Remember my sixth-grader who had an unsuccessful classroom experience? We spent hours on homework, but he still struggled, and the school dictated our schedule. A mother of ten recently told me she would never be able to send her children to school; her life would be much more complicated dealing with multiple schools, teachers, and the accompanying activities that would come with each child. Homeschooling was much simpler.

A Family First

The real issue isn't how full your family life is, keeping you from doing *all* you think you should do. The heart issue is that being a wife, mother, and homekeeper is a challenging job even if you don't home teach; and the choices you make about how to manage your home and train your children remain the same whether or not you homeschool.

You are a family, not a school. You are a mom (or dad), not a schoolteacher. Your children will remember more about the relationships in your family than they will about the academic lessons you brilliantly produce. You can't personally teach them everything they will learn in life, even if you teach them how to learn and where to go to learn further. Neither can an institution. However, the story of your family stays with them all their lives. Some parents will do a better job of "educating" their children than others, but that education is only worthwhile if parents teach the values, attitudes, character, habits, and life skills that children need in order to develop as adults.

> A family is a formation center for human relationships. . . . The place where the deep understanding that people are significant, important, worthwhile, with a purpose in life, should be learned at an early age.
>
> —Edith Schaeffer, *What Is a Family?*

In my early attempts to be a good *teacher* for my sons, I neglected to correlate the important task of becoming the best parent I could be with helping my family become the best family it could be. I missed the point, and the Lord had to teach me.

When we read Scripture, we see how much God values the family. Examples abound: the creation of the first family, the long genealogical lists, the picture of a kinsman-redeemer, God's covenant relationship with families, the careful keeping of family records by clans, the incorporating of servants and strangers into family, the treatment of the family as one unit based on the father's actions (for good or for evil), God's careful selection of a mother (and earthly father) for Jesus, God's description of Himself as Father and the body of Christ as His family, requirements that church leaders manage their families well, and instructions to fathers (and by implication to mothers) on how to teach their children. There are hundreds of references in Scripture for family, father, mother, parents, and children. It is evident that God highly regards His special creation—the family.

The Stress of Disorganization

You probably agree that the family is important; after all, you've chosen to homeschool. However, you might be asking what the importance of the family has to do with organization. Organization helps a family fulfill its mission in life; disorganization is stressful and thus has a negative effect on the family.

In June 1997, Doctor of Education Susan A. McDowell from Vanderbilt University conducted research that resulted in the study titled "The Perceived Impact of Homeschooling on the Family in General and the Mother-Teacher in Particular," published in the National Home Education Research Institute's journal, the *Home School Researcher*.[1] After all the studies about homeschool children, how they learn, what backgrounds they come from, how well socialized they are, ad infinitum, mothers finally have their own study!

Dr. McDowell administered a survey to 125 homeschooling moms attending the 11th Annual Family Resource Fair in Knoxville, Tennessee, to find out the answer to the question about "the perceived impact of homeschooling on the family in general and the mother in particular" and to discover the perceived stressors presented to the study participants in a portion of the study. According to the data, "the item clearly found to be the most stress-inducing by respondents was 'lack of organization,'" with housework the second and related cause. Concerns about children learning, financial issues, choosing a curriculum, and using good teaching methods ranked below organization and housework concerns. Most of us can relate to the study outcome.

There can be a domino effect: Mom is not organized or has difficulty inducing the family's cooperation with organization, causing stress; Mom's stress affects the family; home and school suffer and are chaotic; family relationships become tense and slowly erode; and the family breaks down (blaming the trouble on homeschooling). In fact, the trouble may not be homeschooling at all, but rather the battle—prodded by sinful natures—that families fight in order to get organized.

Organization is a family responsibility, emanating from Mom and Dad but carried out with cooperation from the whole family. Remember the definition? (See page 3.) Organization is about choices—choices that pertain to making life function better for God's glory by the wise use of time, guided by the Holy Spirit, because we have relief from the dailiness-of-life pressures.

Unless the LORD builds a house, its builders labor over it in vain.

—*Psalm 127:1*

If your family were not homeschooling, would disorganization be an issue? While it's true that there would be less daytime activity, probably easing some stress, other family difficulties would continue because of disorganization. Your family would simply exchange the stress of homeschooling for such stress factors as dealing with schools and teachers, and the disorganization would remain. Homeschooling is not necessarily the cause of all family disruptions; it only exposes inherent difficulties. Organization, or the lack of it, does impact family relationships, often in undetected ways.

Purposeful Family Life

Recently I encountered the word *stochastic*. It's an adjective that means lacking any definite plan, order, or purpose; depending on or governed by chance. Stochastic is the opposite of how God designed our families to function.

Purposeful family living relates to organization that relates to self-discipline that relates to diligence that relates to commitment. Self-discipline is a mutual effort between the indwelling Holy Spirit and our will yielded to God's authority—something in which we all can improve. The path is not the end; it is the means. To be the family God has designed, we must have commitment; but commitment won't take us anywhere without diligence in the means to get there. Diligence requires self-discipline or self-control (a fruit of the Spirit, Galatians 5:22–23) that leads to organization in the best sense of the word—those choices we make—which produces purposeful family living that gives glory to God.

There can be no greater vocation in life than the family responsibility of sharing life with the growing child. The school is an extension of our home. It doesn't "just happen." Stop and think. Get priorities right.

—Susan Schaeffer Macaulay, *For the Children's Sake*

When haphazardness characterizes our families, tempers flare, miscommunications occur, and life is chaotic. Disorder diverts us from purposeful family living. Since God demonstrates that He is a God of order, neglect does not reflect the image of Christ's body that it should. Children do not thrive, grow, and learn as well in a disorganized atmosphere, and they don't learn practical life skills that help them along their way.

By this point you know that I'm not speaking of perfect families; there are none. Your family is different from mine and from others. God created uniqueness in your family unit and its individuals as cause for celebration. Nevertheless, the underlying principle of order and organization should form a foundation for every Christian family. One mom related to me that the way she explains the family schedule to her children is by telling them, "It's like the law (God's law)—we can't keep it perfectly, but it's our guide, and we strive to follow it."

I don't know the ways disorganization has affected your family, but I'm sure you are aware of them. Possibly you have lost valuable items that cost precious family income to replace. Maybe a family member's anger has caused hurt and pain when chaos resulted in miscommunication. Perhaps someone in the family misplaced important papers, causing wasted time, inconvenience, and the need for replacement. Family members being late or unprepared due to disorder may have caused a missed opportunity, minor or important. Whether the consequences of disorganization are small or of greater import, they affect you, your spouse, and your children in ways that keep you from fulfilling God's greater purpose in your lives.

If you have experienced the effects of disorganization, I want to encourage you. God teaches us through our failures and urges us to draw near to Him as He forms us into the image of His precious Son. He uses external things in our lives to point to the internal remolding He is doing. God's mercies are new every morning, and His faithfulness abounds (Lamentations 3:22–24). We can look with expectancy and hope to the work He is doing in us and in our families as we allow Him to mold us like clay (Isaiah 64:4–8).

Extended Family Relationships

Exploring the details of relationships between a homeschooling family and grandparents is beyond the scope of this book, but I believe it is the homeschooling family's responsibility to do everything possible to nurture and promote the relationship. Grandparents often have concerns when they see you struggling to function effectively as you home teach. Their response frequently is to blame homeschooling. In the face of hostility, there is usually the lack of proper understanding between families.

You may or may not have the benefit of grandparents who support your effort and even help you in those endeavors, but God—the God of generations—places importance on your relationship with grandparents and extended family. No, it doesn't take a village to raise a child, but I believe it is God's ideal for homeschooling and parenting to embrace the support of the extended family—grandparents, aunts, uncles, and others.

You may have heard it said that homeschooling is a family restoration movement, and you may be experiencing the blessings of better unity and purpose in your family and extended family. However, when there are differences between family members, it is beneficial to remember that home education is different from what immediate past generations chose. While it has a long history, it is revolutionary in our time. Our decision and attitude about homeschooling our children can make grandparents and other family members feel judged, inadequate, and resentful. God desires to teach each of us about His love, grace, and mercy through our extended families. The responsibility begins with the homeschooling family to bridge that gap ("If possible, on your part, live at peace with everyone," Romans 12:18).

The decision to homeschool is not one
that should be made lightly, yet with
the Lord's guidance and direction we
can remain faithful to His calling
even through rough circumstances like
family resistance.

—Debbie Strayer, *Gaining Confidence to Teach*

Grandparents Can Help

Because the extended family is important, there are ways that grandparents
can support your homeschooling efforts—more accurately your family development efforts—and help ease your struggle in various ways. There are many
"do's" and some "don'ts" for grandparents to implement in order to be a positive
influence and help to the family. You may wish to share this book or just this
chapter with grandparents, if you have a positive relationship with them, but you
can also share the ideas even if you don't give them the book. If your children do
not have helpful or cooperative grandparents, pray that God will provide a new
understanding of homeschooling and of how you want to raise your children.

Grandparents,*

Do pray for your children and grandchildren if you are a Christian. They
need your prayers more than anything you can give them.

Do listen to your children to hear their hearts' desire to be good parents and
do the best for their children rather than following the popular culture.

* Homeschooling parents and grandparents have shared all of these suggestions with me, or I have gleaned
them from my grandparenting experiences.

Do read resources your children share with you or attend a homeschool conference with them if you are able. Grandparents' admission is free at most conferences.

Do try to understand what they are doing. Let them be wrong if necessary. Go back to the first suggestion and pray for them. That is one of the hardest things a parent can do, isn't it?

Do ask for your children's approval before buying electronics, games, and movies for *their* children. Every family has its own sensitivities when it comes to appropriateness. Remember that the culture is rapidly declining and kid entertainment isn't the same as it was when you were a child or even when your children were young.

Do praise them where you can. Remember how things were when you had young children at home.

Do remember that they may be carrying a financial burden and making sacrifices. Having Mom at home will be a blessing to the children, and the children won't notice any lack when they have the privilege of a stay-at-home mom.

Do respect their differences with you. God is able to convict them about what they should do, and God won't waste any of their decisions, right or wrong.

Do save your concerns to discuss with your children, not your grandchildren. Your grandchildren will resent you if you constantly criticize their parents or use them to make your point to their parents.

Do support your children's rules for your grandchildren, even if you disagree, and enforce those rules and principles when the grandchildren are with you.

One of the beauties of homeschooling is that it allows us to recognize and nurture each one of our very special individual children.

—Cathy Duffy, *100 Top Picks*

Do be an example and retain your identity as their elder. You know things about life that they don't know yet. Be a grandparent, loving and teaching them, and not just a buddy to the grandchildren. Grandchildren will often talk to grandparents about things that are bothering them, if there is a good relationship.

Do share your past with your grandchildren by keeping a notebook or writing letters to them about your childhood. You are the important connection to the past for your grandchildren enabling them to understand their future. (Mom, you might let your children make a mailbox from a shoebox for letters they receive.)

Do send audio- and videotapes and pictures, if you live away. My favorite tape is one in which my oldest grandson is playing the piano when he was a beginner.

Do take your grandchildren on trips, if you are able. One widow I know takes one grandchild per year on a trip with her for one-on-one time.

Do ask for a wish list from your children for gift giving and for extras that aren't in their budget. Mom and Dad appreciate the children's receiving quality educational things rather than fad toys.

Do teach a class or skill to your grandchildren or to a group of homeschooling children. One great-grandfather taught basket weaving to a group. Teach the skills you know may disappear in the next generations if you don't pass them along.

Do help, when time and health allow, with local or state support groups. They welcome grandparents who will stuff envelopes, type, make calls, or answer phones. People involved in leadership often are home-teaching parents and bear a heavy load to serve their fellow homeschoolers.

By contrast [to textbooks], real people write the real books, people with opinions and interesting things to say, whether fiction or nonfiction.

—Ruth Beechick, *Homeschooling Methods*

Do take the grandchildren shopping or on field trips if your time and strength allow. One of my fondest memories is of my grandmother taking me to the Salvation Army thrift store to buy dress-up clothes and taking me to lunch and shopping on my birthday.

Do adapt your visits to the family's schedule, if possible. They may need to get to a particular stopping place in their studies so they can relax and enjoy your visit, particularly if the visit is extended because you are traveling from another town.

Do read to your grandchildren and tell stories. Reading to them is one of the best ways to help children learn to read. Besides, it's fun!

Do help with the household, if you live nearby, as you are able and as the family wishes. Cook, bake, clean with the grandchildren, and teach them to work. Mom will appreciate the help! One friend has a weekly Grandparents Day when the grandparents come to her home and help in any way needed, including teaching. The children look forward to the day as they are going about their normal routine with the grandparents there to interact with them.

Do babysit when possible. Set ground rules for clear understandings. The family should not impose with expectations of instant babysitting, and grandparents should not be martyrs and not say no when they need to. Sometimes Mom just needs someone to watch the children while she takes a nap. One mother at a conference told me, in tears, that her mother thought it was terrible that she had so many children, and she refused to help her daughter.

Do anything you are able to do to be a part of your children's lives that will help them raise, love, and educate their children—your precious grandchildren—who are the next generation of God's children.

Now some "don'ts"—

Don't buy curriculum unless Mom and Dad approve your choices.

Don't try to bail them out of every financial crisis. God teaches through sacrifice at times. Likewise, don't buy the grandchildren too many toys or entertainment-related items, and don't take them only to amusements parks. Instead, look for fun learning experiences for them.

Don't give advice if you do not have a good relationship with your children. Mature families usually ask for advice from grandparents, but that depends upon the relationship.

Don't expect perfection from their homeschooling or child rearing. You weren't perfect either.

Don't give up on your children. They need you and you need them! You are making a mark on eternity as well as your posterity. How do you want your grandchildren to remember you?

A man's heart plans his way, but the
LORD determines his steps.

—*Proverbs 16:9*

An Exhortation

Homeschooling has the potential to bring families together while they learn and grow in life situations. Living and learning in a family context creates a desire in children to learn what real life is about. If you are discouraged or thinking of abandoning homeschooling because it is hard, I want to encourage you.

I exhort you to discover the real reasons it seems hard. It may not be because of home teaching. God has a plan for your family, and it could include the lessons you learn from being a family rather than a "school"—lessons that you and your children can't learn in a book!

After you work through the exercises, let's look at organization beyond the family, in service to others through hospitality.

Stop, Look, Think

Direction—Where Are You Going?

1. Has lack of organization caused you and your family stress in some way? List any ways that weaknesses in organization skills have produced negative results in your life and family. Are you willing to apply helpful principles to make needed changes?

2. Have you been putting more effort into being a teacher than in being a mom and home-keeper? What do you need to change?

3. In what ways have organization skills helped you be a family rather than a school?

4. If it is appropriate in your extended family situation, share with grandparents the ideas and ways they can help. Add any of your own that aren't on the list.

Devotion—What Are You Thinking?

1. Have you been guilty of making excuses and blaming homeschooling or the children for personal struggles? Confess those to the Lord, and ask Him to show you how to achieve balance in your home for His honor and glory. Read Philippians 4:13. While this refers to being content with plenty or little, it certainly applies to being content with our circumstances as well.

2. Ask the Lord to show you wrong attitudes, motives, and actions in you or your children that homeschooling or disorganization has exposed. Praise Him that you want to bring your family to maturity to glorify Him. Read Isaiah 64:4–8; 1 Corinthians 9:24–26; Hebrews 12:7–11; and 2 Peter 1:5–7.

3. Read Lamentations 3:22–24 and Philippians 1:6 and thank the Lord that He is doing His work in you and your family and He will complete that work. Write a prayer of thanks to the Lord. You might put this prayer in a journal or write it out on a three-by-five card and place it where you can see it; your own words can remind you to be thankful.

Notes

Chapter 9

A Hospitable Home

I think Martha gets a bum rap! No, I'm not referring to the conviction and jail term of *the* Martha Stewart, homemaker extraordinaire of television fame. I mean the Martha in Luke 10:38–42.

While they were traveling, He [Jesus] entered a village, and a woman named Martha welcomed Him into her home. She had a sister named Mary, who also sat at the Lord's feet and was listening to what He said. But Martha was distracted by her many tasks, and she came up and asked, "Lord, don't You care that my sister has left me to serve alone? So tell her to give me a hand." The Lord answered her, "Martha, Martha, you are worried and upset about many things, but one thing is necessary. Mary has made the right choice, and it will not be taken away from her."

We see Martha bustling about, busy with serving and preparations, and her sister, Mary, sitting at Jesus' feet listening to Him. When Jesus tenderly scolds Martha because of her complaints that Mary isn't helping her, we tend to side with Mary (Who of us wouldn't rather be at Jesus' feet listening?), and we see Martha's glaring faults. Isn't Jesus telling Martha to stop her preparations, sit down, and join Mary?

I'm not a Bible scholar, but I believe Jesus aimed at least part of His rebuke at Martha's complaints rather than her preparations. We make preparations in everyday life, but our heart attitude about those preparations sometimes needs examination. It appears, though Scripture doesn't tell us specifically, that Jesus didn't address her about her hustle and bustle until she began urging Him to tell Mary to help with the work. She was focusing on herself and on having to serve alone when she complained. Her heart was not joyfully serving her guests in her circumstances, and she wasn't following Peter's encouragement in 1 Peter 4:9. "Be hospitable to one another without complaining." Jesus looks at her heart—and at ours.

Genuine Hospitality

My family has lived in eleven different cities in four states over thirty-six years. In each new place we have longed for warm hospitality. Those who shared with us became lifelong friends, even after we left their city. Some were blessed with beautiful, expensive homes; and others simply used the humble resources the Lord had given them to serve us. However, they all had one thing in common: they had open, warm homes that reflected their warm hearts.

Who is the most hospitable person you have known? What sights, smells, sounds, and feelings come to mind when you think of being in that person's home? Do you remember the smell of delicious food wafting through the air and beckoning from the front door? Was the home orderly, making you comfortable sitting in the living room with a cup of tea or coffee and engaging in interesting conversation? Was nice music playing softly in the background or did you hear happy sounds of laughter? Did someone greet you warmly when you arrived, with an offer of refreshment while dinner preparations were completed? Did you feel welcomed?

Based on our background, we envision different pictures of genuine hospitality, but probably we don't remember fine china, a perfect home, or even a five-course gourmet meal. Doesn't your memory take you back to the warmth of the fellowship and the attention of your host and hostess as they ensured your comfort and care? Be it ever so humble, isn't it the feeling of *home* that makes you fondly recall occasions of genuine hospitality?

There are strange ways of serving God; You sweep a room or turn a sod, And suddenly, to your surprise, You hear the whirr of seraphim, And find you're under God's own eyes And building palaces for Him.

—Herman Hagedorn, *Little Things*

Scripture and my experience lead me to conclude that true hospitality consists of who you are and not what you have. Hospitality isn't producing a magazine-cover home with expensive place settings and a gourmet meal. It certainly isn't a game of one-upmanship, seeing if you can outdo your hostess when you invite her to your home. It is the love and care that you show others when you open your home to them, sharing the Lord's love that flows there. When you are hospitable, you are obedient to the Lord, as Scripture directs us (Romans 12:13; Hebrews 13:2—even widows and leaders are judged by their record of hospitality; 1 Timothy 5:9–10; Titus 1:8).

Understanding that hospitality is a way of life and knowing that the Lord wants you to obey Him does not mean that you know how to go about it. Perhaps you have had frustrating experiences as a hostess. The new recipe you tried was a failure, you rushed getting the house clean before guests arrived, or you felt awkward because your home was not as large or as elegant as you would like. The acronym, GUEST, may help you and your family think of the components of being a good hostess or host. Let's look at the initial letters in the acronym.

Only by His grace can we find the
will to organize our time and material
possessions in ways which minister to
those around us and allow us to fulfil
our life purpose in Him.

—Terry Dorian, *Anyone Can Homeschool*

Give Graciously

Before thinking about setting a nice table, cooking a good meal for guests, or learning new entertainment tips, cultivate a gracious and joyful heart that is focused on others—those whom the Lord sends across your threshold. Heart attitudes show; it is hard to hide resentment or a perfectionistic attitude when you entertain others in your home. People instinctively know if you sincerely want them there, and they quickly overlook imperfections in your home if you warmly give attention to their needs.

Do you feel that your home is inadequate in quality or size, and therefore you don't invite guests? Do you make excuses because you don't feel organized enough to have company? Have you wanted to invite a new friend or maybe a new family that attends your church for an occasion with your family, but you can't seem to make the time? Set aside your excuses and let your guests be the focus in your hospitable home. Give them yourself, not just your home.

Understand Usual Needs

Some hostesses gladly open their homes, but they are so casual toward guests that they don't communicate a proper care and concern for the guests' needs. I have been in homes where the hostess was attempting to make me feel comfortable by simply saying, "Make yourself at home," and I'm sure her intent was genuine. However, a guest seldom feels free to go looking for needs in the kitchen or bathroom cabinets without some direction. In her attempt to make a guest feel welcome, the hostess makes the guest feel ill at ease.

Try to anticipate your guests' requirements. If you have overnight guests, provide extras of such necessities as toothpaste, toothbrush, hand lotion, shampoo, deodorant, disposable razor, and shave cream. A tiny sewing kit with safety pins comes in handy; and small, hotel-size soaps are nice for guests to shower with their own soap. If you put these things into a pretty basket and place it in the guests' room, they will feel pampered. Lay out towels and washcloths especially for guests rather than have them guess which ones hanging in the bathroom they should use. If they share a bath with children in your family, either bring the children temporarily into your bath, giving the guests some privacy, or be sure you train your children well to leave the bathroom neat and clean for the guests.

> Share with the saints in their needs;
> pursue hospitality.
>
> —*Romans 12:13*

A water carafe or small pitcher and glass are nice at the bedside, along with a few mints. Adequate light for reading, a couple of books—maybe a devotional or something short and interesting—possibly a radio or tape/CD player with a variety of music, an alarm clock, and a small Bible are lovely additions. Snacks and beverage glasses on a tray in the kitchen with instructions to help themselves are nice. A nightlight in the kitchen, hall, and bathroom are helpful if a guest has to leave the bedroom during the night. Think of articles you need or enjoy having when you are away from home.

Many families don't have a guest room that is unused by family members. Having overnight guests sometimes necessitates that one or more of the children give up their bedrooms. My boys considered it an adventure when they were able to sleep on the couch or in sleeping bags on the floor while guests occupied their bedrooms. Be sure to put clean linens and covers on the bed that the guest will use. Pick up toys and children's possessions and make the room as neat as possible. Push clothes aside in the closet and provide a few hangers for hanging clothes. If you have room, you could provide one empty drawer for guests who stay several days. A luggage rack for the guest's suitcase is a special treat; and if you are unable to purchase one, Dad and the kids may be able to make one that is suitable and that folds away when not needed.

A generous person will be enriched, and the one who gives a drink of water will receive water.

—Proverbs 11:25

If guests are in your home for a day or an evening, be sure they know where the restroom is located and direct them to the most comfortable seating in your living or family room. Plan ahead so you can actually spend time with your guests rather than continually excusing yourself for meal or snack preparations. Remember that they are there to see you, and it is embarrassing for them if you are up and down numerous times rather than fellowshipping with them. Of course, if your guests are family or good friends, they may be in the kitchen with you getting dinner on the table, but even then you need a simple meal that is almost finished when guests arrive.

I'll never forget the time, a number of years ago, that I traveled to another city to speak at a homeschool conference. Various families were housing the speakers, and I spent the night on a family's couch bed in the middle of their open living room downstairs, with the children snug in their beds upstairs. I had a rather sleepless night wondering if a family member might venture downstairs at an embarrassing moment. To make matters worse, there was no downstairs bathroom; the bathroom was upstairs near all the bedrooms.

The family was kind to open their home to me, and I'm sure they had good intentions. However, they had not developed the heart-eye to see their guests' needs. Look at your home from guests' perspectives to understand what they might require for comfort.

> # Don't neglect to show hospitality, for by doing this some have welcomed angels as guests without knowing it.
>
> *—Hebrews 13:2*

Educate for Etiquette

Is the behavior of your children a deterrent to happy, joyful entertaining? Practice a nice meal without guests but with all the proper silverware and place settings. Teach everyone how to properly pass food at the table and to offer dishes to others before taking a portion for themselves. Teach your young men to pull out a chair for a lady. Dress up for dinner. Your valuable instruction now, in the safe and caring setting of your home, will save unnecessary embarrassment when children are in public or at someone else's home for dinner. Additionally, is there any reason your family shouldn't practice most of these good table manners in your home every day?

It takes your constant instruction on a routine basis to teach children to sit up to the table, not stand up in their chairs, keep their elbows off the table, chew their food well, not talk with their mouths full, and generally be polite. Practice doesn't make perfect; only perfect practice makes perfect. If you only expect good manners during company situations, children won't remember how they are to behave at other times. You may feel like a broken record or a scratched CD at times, continually reminding your children about their manners, but this is an important long-term effort. Young adults who reach eighteen and still don't know or recognize proper etiquette will experience life hindrances. Remember the question in chapter 4: If I don't teach _____, will the lack of that knowledge be harmful or a hindrance to them later in life?

> # We will never arrive at the state of being a perfect person or a perfect family ready to share something of our "perfect home."
>
> —Edith Schaeffer, *What Is a Family?*

Perhaps good etiquette wasn't part of your early training. If not, buy a good etiquette book and learn with your children. Good manners books specifically for children are available at various online bookstores. The most important rule of good etiquette—more important than which fork to use—is always to think of the other person's needs. Do what makes someone else comfortable, and you will rarely go wrong.

Simplify Your System

Simplicity is the best policy for entertainment and hospitality. If you keep it simple, you will want to have guests often. Entertaining doesn't have to be a big event. You will give up without even bothering to invite others to your home if you feel you must have an elaborate meal or a fancy dessert or that your home must be perfectly in order. You will be replacing the *joy* of friends with the *job* of entertaining.

I recall the story recounted to me by a friend who was counseling a struggling homeschool family. The mother was so obsessed with having a perfect home that each time they were to entertain guests she demanded that her daughters clean the house from top to bottom, even in the nonpublic areas of the home where company would not venture and even if they had just cleaned it recently. Because of the mother's demanding, perfectionistic attitude, the daughters resented their mother, and tension between them was building. Obviously, rather than real joy in anticipation of guests, the mother focused on her image. While a dirty and disheveled home isn't inviting to guests, they usually don't notice small things that only you know are there. Clean the public areas of your home well, and don't sweat the small stuff!

Have you been guilty of trying out a new recipe on guests? I have, and it can be a recipe for disaster! Keep a list of a few simple, do-ahead meals to choose from when you are having company. Do you make the best Texas chili in the neighborhood? Does everyone rave about your lasagna? Do you love backyard cooking on the grill? Whatever you choose, make it something that is a tried-and-true favorite for everyone. If you don't know your guests well, it is wise to ask them ahead of time if they have food allergies or special dislikes. I almost had a disaster when I prepared shrimp gumbo and found out just a few hours before guests arrived that one of them was allergic to shrimp! Fortunately, I simply divided the gumbo before I added the shrimp and used chicken for my guest's portion. I could have avoided the near disaster by asking beforehand.

Keep choices to a minimum. Choosing from five drinks is overwhelming! When tempted to add one more item to the menu, don't. Have plenty of a few things.

Keep it simple by cleaning the house, if needed, the day before so that all you and your family need do is quickly pick up before people arrive. They seldom notice a little dust, but a cluttered home makes for uncomfortable guests. Enter the front door of your home with an eye for how it appears to others; does it say *welcome* to people in some way?

Set the table well ahead of mealtime, perhaps right after lunch if company is coming for the evening meal. Think of everything needed for the meal—dressing for salad, butter for bread, salt and pepper on the table. Just before guests arrive, light a nice scented candle, out of the reach of little ones, and put on pleasant, quiet background music. Use the List Minder in this book's CD to record all the things you need to remember and check them off or have your children check them off as someone does them.

If a full meal for guests seems too overwhelming for your current circumstances, don't let that stop you from obeying the Lord's command for hospitality. Invite someone over for dessert or popcorn and games. Take a picnic dinner to the park and invite another family to go with you. Don't let a dreaded meal preparation keep you from enjoying friends and ministering to people, which is the true focus of hospitality. If you simplify your system, you will find it much easier and enjoyable to welcome guests into your home.

Take Time

I grew up in the land of hospitality—the South. I'm now a grandmother, so I'm old enough to remember polite manners, good home-cooked food, Sunday dinner—that's lunch for those not raised in the South—starched linens and fine china on the table, and the family's best for company. Company came frequently and almost every woman knew how to entertain well.

> If I can put one touch of rosy
> sunset into the life of any man
> or woman, I shall feel that I have
> worked with God.
>
> —George MacDonald, *Little Things*

Today paper plates are the norm for a crowd, the family is too busy to issue frequent invitations, and Sunday dinner often takes place in a local restaurant, if at all. While I'm the first to admit that all the fuss and preparation of those bygone days were, at times, an unnecessary show, I wonder if the true heart of hospitality has slipped quietly away from our culture. As people drift farther apart, families are falling apart.

In a 2004 study that paralleled a similar study in 1985, the number of Americans who considered themselves isolated—meaning there was no one with whom to discuss personal troubles—more than doubled. In just twenty years the number of people who said they counted a neighbor as a confidant dropped from about 19 percent to around 8 percent—more than half, and the number was already low.[1]

The study results showing such a steep decline in close social ties surprised researchers, but it shouldn't surprise us. We see it and feel it around us. Even the body of Christ, who should be reaching out to others, is guilty. In the past our family has been part of a church for as long as two years and never been invited to anyone's home for any reason.

Homeschoolers desire to return to the center of family living and have the opportunity to restore the fading art of hospitality. We have the opportunity to show our children a picture of loving others by bringing them into the intimate parts of our life—into our homes. We have the blessing of being able to minister to another homeschool family by mentoring them and being there for a while as they start to homeschool. We have the occasion to minister to people around us who feel isolated and alone. We have the option to share the hope that is in us (1 Peter 3:14–16) by bringing people into our homes to love them. When people know we care about them by the way we express our concern, they will know more about the God who loves His creation and wants to restore people to His kingdom. We may be the only visible demonstration of that love to some people.

In the dedication of Karen Santorum's lovely book *Everyday Graces: A Child's Book of Good Manners*, she thanks her children and says that she hopes they may grow up to be kind and caring adults who see the joy in serving others. Mrs. Santorum has identified the heart of hospitality.

If our homes and families are no different from those of nonhomeschoolers, what good reasons do we present for homeschooling? Other Christians, and sometimes non-Christians, instinctively want what we have; but they should see the correct picture as an example—not to become a clone of *our* homes but to see the picture of a home filled with acceptance of others, love, peace, laughter, and learning that welcomes others into the circle.

If your desire is to make your home a peaceful and loving place where others are welcome at your hearth, I encourage you to start small but begin to make the necessary changes to accomplish that biblical goal. Add your desires to your family mission statement and to your goals sheet. Make a plan that is workable for your family and begin. Who knows, you may even contribute to bringing back the good old days of civil culture and good manners, even if it is on paper plates.

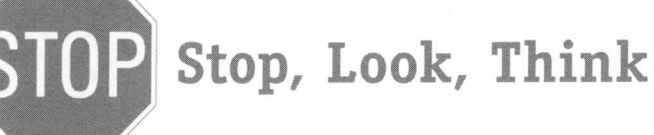

STOP Stop, Look, Think

Direction—Where Are You Going?

1. List normal home-keeping practices that you feel prevent you from offering hospitality. Do you invite guests to your home regularly? If not,

make a plan to begin practicing hospitality that is doable for you and your family. Begin simple!

2. Even if you invite guests frequently, is there a GUEST area in which you need to improve? (Give Graciously, Understand Usual Needs, Educate for Etiquette, Simplify Your System, and Take Time). Examine these areas and your list in question 1 and make changes or additions as needed. Make them part of your regular routine

3. Concentrate on teaching your children good manners. Really observe your children to see what they need to learn. List things you want to teach them and work on a few at a time. Make it fun—have an elbows-off-the-table-week, a napkin-in-the-lap month, or a funny penalty for talking with your mouth full—and give prizes for those who accomplish the expected behavior. Use your creativity!

Devotion—What Are You Thinking?

1. Ask the Lord to examine your heart in this area of genuine hospitality. Are you giving graciously, both inside and outside your home? Write your thoughts about what you understand you should do to obey.

2. Read the Scriptures mentioned in this chapter: Romans 12:13; 1 Timothy 5:9–10; Titus 1:8; 1 Peter 4:9; Hebrews 13:2. Are you obedient to the Lord in these areas? Ask Him to help you move toward obedience in your family.

3. Has the Lord placed someone on your heart to reach out to but you haven't taken the time to do so? Ask the Lord to open your eyes to an opportunity to show hospitality and love to that person. Involve the whole family, if appropriate.

4. Ask the Lord if there is a way you can serve as a family in your church rather than divided in various ways. If you see a need, talk to those in leadership about your family service.

Notes

Chapter 10

Finishing Well

What if you could do it all? You can't, of course, but let's dream a minute. What would your home look like? How would your family function? What would your school day consist of? What would you love to do with your children?

When your children are young, it's difficult to imagine years ahead. It's hard to picture those chubby, sweet cheeks and those mischievous eyes in the head of a grown man. It's extremely hard to think of your little ones grown, married, and on their own. Those future days seem impossibly far away when you're chasing a toddler, nursing an ear infection, unstopping flushed Legos from the toilet and mopping up muddy footprints (again) from the kitchen floor.

Life speeds by, and those footprints grow much too quickly. After fifteen years, I ran out of sons to teach—just when I was getting the hang of homeschooling. Looking back, I now know there are some things I would have done differently: I would have dared more; I would have listened more; and I would have read more, even though I thought we read a lot. I also would have prayed more if I had known all that was ahead, and I would have trusted God more for the outcome.

Yes, the *outcome* is down the road for all of us. It's where you're going now with your children. You can't see that outcome; you travel by faith. The time goes quickly. As I write, my youngest son's wedding is only two months away. This is my son who didn't read until he was nine years old. By the time he was sixteen years old, he had nineteen college credits. He graduated from a prestigious, four-year private college. Impossible as it seems now, he is getting married at twenty-seven to a beautiful, godly young woman.

In gathering information for this book, I contacted homeschool mothers who were fellow travelers while we home taught. I wanted to hear what they had to say on the praise end of their homeschooling days. In every case they said similar things about how fast the time went, how grateful they were that they homeschooled, how there were days when they wanted to quit, how much they learned from homeschooling, and how hard it was at times. I concur with everything they said.

One of the moms I talked with who still has one more child at home, and who particularly struggled through years of homeschooling, just saw her oldest son graduate from college and marry the following week. He is a fine, godly young man, and the Lord brought him a lovely, godly wife. When I asked my friend if she could see this outcome during those hard years, she said, "No. Tell your readers that God is faithful; that's what they need to know. God is faithful!"

He who calls you is faithful, who also will do it.

—1 Thessalonians 5:24

She's right. Don't we often have the mistaken idea that it is our job to finish training our children? God gives us the privilege of training them in the beginning; it is God who finishes what He wants to accomplish in them. Philippians 1:6 says, "I am sure of this, that He who started a good work in you will carry it on to completion until the day of Christ Jesus."

The outcome isn't always what we expect or necessarily what we want. Life moves fast and it's messy, even when children aren't toddlers any longer. We survive through hard times, tears, laughter, disagreements, joys, work, accomplishments, prayer, and praise all mixed together to form our unique family. Nevertheless, we can be sure that the outcome is what God has designed. Certainly, we are to do our part, and we will by God's grace, but He is the author and finisher of each of us, including our children.

Our Part

Organization in the home and our responsibility as parents are difficult to separate; the two are intrinsically connected. Every homeschool mother has days when she asks, "Now, why am I homeschooling?" and those struggles are often connected to balancing the task of home-keeping with teaching. It's difficult to remember, in the dailiness of life, why we are doing it. Then the kids remind us.

One mom e-mailed me that she has four boys under the age of seven. Her days are full, and she does many juggling acts, but she is beginning well. She shared that her boys are all best friends and play together. The five-year-old calls his seven-year-old brother his "bestest brother." The seven-year-old commented that he probably wouldn't want to go to school because he "wouldn't get to be with all of you as much. I would miss you." This mom is seeing the way God designed sibling relationships. She said, "I really enjoy being the one who gets to teach them the academics, but one of the greatest joys my husband and I experience is watching them play, imagine, interact, and love one another the way the Lord intended brothers to relate."

Ten or twelve years from now will this young mother know that she finished well? Will you? What is your part? How *do* you finish well? Perhaps condensing a few thoughts will balance the ideas in the preceding chapters. Let's look at four principles for finishing well: pray, plan, pool your resources, and persevere.

I am the vine; you are the branches.
The one who remains in Me and I in
him produces much fruit, because you
can do nothing without Me.

—John 15:5

Pray

While homeschooling my children, I earned my PhD—that stands for Praying for Help Daily! Christian homeschool moms know better than almost anyone that they are dependent on the Lord and that He is their strength. All the wonderful things God has for you in the adventure of homeschooling come with God; it's a package deal. Stay close to Him if you want to finish well. He is your true School Supply Source, and He is the one who knows and directs that illusive "perfect" curriculum you are always searching for.

Are you talking to and, most important, listening to God—going to Him for your needs, confessing your faults, asking Him for His mercy, thanking Him for grace to raise and teach your children, and depending on Him for everything you need? For wisdom? For financial needs? For diligence in your duties? For physical and emotional strength? You'll forget at times who your Source is, but continually pray for Him to draw you back. He will do that because He wants the best outcome more than you do.

Plan

One mom shared with me that she and her homeschool-mom-best-friend have a saying: "At the end of the day, if the house looks great and dinner is ready, we had a bad homeschool day. If, on the other hand, at the end of the day the house is in shambles and dinner is not ready, it must have been a great school day!" This mom expresses the conflict many homeschoolers face between equally important tasks. Learning to blend the two is a perpetual process; some days one wins over the other, but we are always seeking balance. Good planning helps us do that more effectively.

Your plans don't always depend on what you want, do they? There are times when your plans are out of your control and you feel as though you are stranded on a mutinous household—uh, ship. One of the reasons God gave you children and asked you to teach them at home is so you would learn to trust Him in a way you wouldn't otherwise.

I can always gauge how well I am trusting God by my reaction when He changes my plans. I recall a time when out-of-town friends—a large family—were coming to stay for about a week. I was running behind with all that I needed to do before they arrived, and I had pushed my grocery shopping for the crowd further and further out. The guests were to arrive the following day, so I had to shop late at the twenty-four-hour store near my home rather than at my favorite store farther away. Off I went, leaving the boys with my husband, who put them to bed. He had an early morning appointment the next day so he, too, had gone to bed by the time I got home with my load.

> I regarded some work as important and other work as menial. . . . Nowhere in the Word of God are we told to consider work in that way.
>
> —Terry Dorian, *Anyone Can Homeschool*

While I grumbled and lugged sack after sack into the house, I tried to ignore my bitter spirit. *Couldn't he at least have stayed up to help me get the bags into the house?* I began to put groceries away so I could drop my tired body into bed as well. I was almost finished, but as I placed an unopened, commercial-size jar of spaghetti sauce on its side in the refrigerator, the lid *exploded!* Spaghetti sauce went flying—on me, the floor, the walls, the cabinets, and even the back of the refrigerator. With profuse red everywhere, my kitchen resembled a disastrous car wreck on the freeway.

I sat down right in the middle of it all and sobbed. Alone in the quiet kitchen amid the mess, I sensed the Lord saying, "I'm with you, Marilyn. Take a deep breath and praise me. Remember Romans 8:28." As I wiped my tears and picked myself up with red sauce dripping from me and the counters, I said, "Lord, You are my strength. Forgive my bad attitude and cleanse me. I'll obey and trust You."

Rest in God alone, my soul, for my hope comes from Him. He alone is my rock and my salvation, my stronghold; I will not be shaken.

—*Psalm 62:5–6*

Without waking my husband, I quietly changed my gooey clothes, and it occurred to me that no one would believe this huge mess. I grabbed the camera and took pictures—maybe not with the purest of motives—thinking I could get at least a little sympathy from the disaster! I put a worship and praise tape on to play and started cleaning. As I cleaned, the Lord cleaned my heart, and I lifted it in praise to Him. The mess was set aright quickly. Only later did it occur to me that there could have been contaminated sauce in the unopened jar, causing pressure to build. The Lord may have protected us from food poisoning.

Oh, and what about the pictures? My family slept through the entire fiasco, but I showed them my lesson in praise. I purchased a refrigerator magnet that said, "Move from panic to praise!" that for a long time held one of those pictures on my refrigerator to remind me of my "spaghetti sauce night" and the Lord's faithfulness to teach me to respond by trusting Him when my plans don't go well.

I encourage you to use what you learn about planning, but trust the Lord. Plan, but hold the plans loosely, and accept your best effort. The Lord will take care of the rest. It is encouraging for me to remember that when Christ was on earth, He didn't heal everyone, perform miracles for everyone, or do everything there was to do to set things right in the world, although He could have done so. However, He did do *everything* that God had for Him to accomplish. His last words on the cross were "It is finished." He is the only one who can speak those words truthfully. Your plans on this earth will never be completely finished. Your essential responsibility is for your personal-from-God-to-do list.

Pool Your Resources

A good friend and head of a homeschool oversight group told me of one mother in the group who, several times during the school year, turned in her paperwork documenting that her son was doing poorly in spelling. Each time she noted that he had repeatedly missed the same words. After several times the poor mother wrote across the paper, "Johnny still failed his spelling test—so sue me!"

> Whatever impact your children will have for God in their generation will be to a great extent shaped by the truths and ideas you plant in their hearts and minds.
>
> —Sally Clarkson, in *Homeschooling Methods*

When you feel as though you have failed in keeping your home or teaching your children, support groups, friends, or a mentor can provide the help and encouragement you need. You may have heard or read the stories about families who lived in the middle of nowhere and the children farmed, studied, and went to Harvard. Yes, there are *some* families like that. However, most families do best when they can pool their resources with other like-minded home educators.

Pooling resources includes teaching your children to work, joining a support group, attending conferences, seeking a veteran homeschool family to mentor you, participating in a teaching co-op, reading good material, talking to other homeschool families, hiring a reliable homeschool teen to help when you need relief, and listening and learning in any way you can. There are many creative ways to pool your resources with others. Choose those that benefit you and your family.

You will have times when you feel as though you failed. Seek help and seek the Lord. Don't buy into the lie that there is a home-educating mom alive who doesn't have struggles. I have spoken with mothers, authors, speakers, and leaders across the country, and *all* have frustrations and even temporary failures.

That brings me to the last principle.

Persevere

Culture says a great deal about success today. Many want it, and few attain it by the world's standard. Some homeschoolers follow after this or that current fad, including curriculum, to try to achieve success, thinking they are doing the best for their children. They sincerely want that outcome. I searched five versions of the Bible for the words *success, successful,* and *successfully.* The greatest number of those words in one version was thirty-five. None of the words appear in the New Testament, and of the thirty-five appearances in the Old Testament, all were instances where success was granted or withheld by God. None mentioned any success that man had achieved for himself.

To operate on the basis of God's call is
to enjoy a great deal of order within.

—Gordon MacDonald, *Ordering Your Private World*

We are clay jars (2 Corinthians 4:7), and God has fashioned us for His pleasure and glory. If you are a believer, you own an amazing possession—the power of choice to love and serve God or to disobey Him. That freedom can be rather frightening, difficult, and full of unknowns. We must walk by the Spirit for God's success in us. When the Galatians deserted their walk, Paul admonished them, "Are you so foolish? After beginning with the Spirit, are you now going to be made complete by the flesh? . . . So then, does God supply you with the Spirit and work miracles among you by the works of the law or by hearing with faith?" (Galatians 3:3, 5).

> Because of the LORD's faithful love we
> do not perish, for His mercies never
> end. They are new every morning;
> great is Your faithfulness! I say:
> The LORD is my portion, therefore
> I will put my hope in Him.
>
> —*Lamentations 3:22–24*

I have a love-hate relationship with change. I look forward to it when I'm dissatisfied with my present circumstances, and I hate it when I'm comfortable and content in my little rut. If you are open to the changes God wants in your life, give up your "if-onlys" and allow Him to order your home and homeschool. He will give you His success. No matter where you are in your home-keeping and homeschooling, with the Lord there is always a new beginning. None of us have *arrived*, but God reminds us to continue to press on and not give up. "Brothers, I do not consider myself to have taken hold of it. But one thing I do: forgetting what is behind and reaching forward to what is ahead, I pursue as my goal the prize promised by God's heavenly call in Christ Jesus" (Philippians 3:13–14).

God will teach you to make wise use of your precariously short time. He teaches you to yield to the Holy Spirit, who brings your daily life under control and produces a life that brings honor and glory to Him. I encourage you to persevere toward that end.

At the beginning of this book, I promised you my prayers. I pray that you are encouraged and renewed to start again or to continue to balance home-keeping and homeschooling. I pray that God will give you strength, diligence, and new insight to believe that your work in your home has eternal consequences. I pray that you will desire the Lord Himself above everything in your life. I also pray that you will live out true organization in your life as you serve your family and those around you.

> *Organization is making your life work for you*
> *by bringing the dailiness of life under control*
> *through yielding to the Holy Spirit*
> *concerning the wise use of your time.*

God is faithful!
Don't stop here; go the extra mile and do the final exercises.

STOP Stop, Look, Think

Direction—Where Are You Going?

1. Decide on one thing you can do as soon as you put this book down that will move you toward a positive change in your home. Write it down and go do it when you finish the rest of these exercises.
2. Has your vision of what you believe God wants you to accomplish changed since you read this book? How?
3. Are you a perfectionist who needs to put down your mop or your school schedule and just go hold your children? If so, on purpose cancel a school day and go to the park or do some other fun activity with the kids.

4. Have you been too indifferent about your duties at home and neglected them because you think homeschooling takes all your time? If so, plan and prepare your husband's favorite meal, or some other activity that would please him, and put your effort for the day into that particular thing.

Devotion—What Are You Thinking?

1. Pray for the Lord to draw you back or to draw you closer to Him. Ask Him to show you the things that are causing you to drift away. Write those things in your notes and recall them occasionally to remind you of your tendency to drift.

2. How have you defined your success of homeschooling or home-keeping? Have you based it on something other than the Lord's desires for you? Read the following Scripture verses and ask the Lord how they apply to you: 2 Chronicles 26:3–5; Job 26:2–3; Proverbs 2:6–8; 3:3–8; 16:20.

3. Tell the Lord honestly where you are right now with your failures, your struggles, and your wrong desires. He knows anyway, so be authentic with Him. Then tell Him how you feel about Him, both positive and negative thoughts. Confess the things that are blocking your relationship with Him. He will call them to your mind if you ask Him (Hosea 14:1–3). Don't make bargains with God. Last, knowing that God loves you, tell Him that you want your relationship with Him to be the first thing in your life—that He is all you need to have joy, peace, the deepest satisfaction, and His success. He is the water and the well. Come to Him to get the only thing that will satisfy your deepest thirst—a relationship with Him. Thank Him for the things He gives you but don't mistake them for the essence of your life. Rest in Him, knowing that other things can't give you your true desires and that He always gives you His best.

May God bless you as you get organized in your home and teach your children . . .

AT THE SPEED OF LIFE!

Notes

Appendix A
Resources

The following resources may help in your efforts to homeschool at the speed of life:

7 Tools for Cultivating Your Child's Potential by Zan Tyler (Nashville, Tenn.: Broadman & Holman Publishers, 2005).

100 Top Picks for Homeschool Curriculum: Choosing the Right Curriculum and Approach for Your Child's Learning Style by Cathy Duffy (Nashville, Tenn.: Broadman & Holman Publishers, 2005).

A Biblical Home Education by Dr. Ruth Beechick (Nashville, Tenn.: B&H Publishing Group, 2007). Other older titles by Dr. Beechick are classics: *The Three R's* (a set of three small books on how to teach math, reading, and language arts), *Dr. Beechick's Homeschool Answer Book*, and *You Can Teach Your Child Successfully* available through many homeschool book retailers.

Anyone Can Homeschool by Terry Dorian, PhD, and Zan Peters Tyler (Lafayette, La.: Huntington House Publishers, 1996).

For the Children's Sake by Susan Schaeffer Macaulay (Wheaton, Ill.: Crossway Books, 1984).

Gaining Confidence to Teach by Debbie Strayer (Melrose, Fla.: Common Sense Press, 1997).

Homeschooling Methods: Seasoned Advice on Learning Styles by multiple authors; general editors, Paul and Gena Suarez (Nashville, Tenn.: Broadman & Holman Publishers, 2006).

Keep a Quiet Heart by Elisabeth Elliot (Grand Rapids, Mich.: Revell, division of Baker Publishing Group, 1995).

Margin by Richard A. Swenson, M.D. (Colorado Springs, Co.: NavPress, 1992).

Organized Kidz by Debbie and David Williams (Houston, Tex.: By the Book Media, 2005).

What Is a Family? by Edith Schaeffer (Old Tappan, N. J.: Fleming H. Revel Co., 1975).

Appendix B
File-a-Plan Category List

1. **Attendance***—attendance forms and records if needed for oversight or state requirements

2. **Catalogs**—homeschool catalogs, brochures, and flyers

3. **Curriculum and Study Plans***—plans for the school year, list of courses and texts/materials, record of curriculum providers and contact information, curriculum for current year, Subject or Unit Worksheet

4. **Field Trips***—brochures, information about potential trips, record of trips taken

5. **Goals***—goals for each family member or student for the year

6. **Grades and Evaluation***—grade or evaluation of each student, report cards, evaluation of each student's strengths/weaknesses

7. **Household***—chore plans, menu plans, master household routine, to-do type forms and plans

8. **Lesson Plans***—lesson plans and record of work completed

9. **Library*** —books read, record of books loaned, list for book search at library, bookstore, or online

10. **Medical and Health Records*** —health records for each family member, doctors' and hospitals' names and addresses, birth certificates (or copies)

11. **Optional Study and Activities** —information on courses outside the home, community college courses, enrichment courses, information on camps, educational seminars, and information on any activities

12. **Organizations*** —support groups, clubs, church groups, sports organizations, political organizations, legal organizations, and so forth

13. **Portfolio and Sample Work*** —portfolio and sample work for each student

14. **Potential Projects*** —projects under consideration, future classes, unit studies, and so forth

15. **Required Forms (State or Oversight)** —oversight forms required by state or oversight group

16. **Testing*** —standardized test results, special needs testing, SAT, ACT, any information about tests

17. **Transcripts*** —student transcripts

18. **Work or Career Planning*** —information about work or careers, student résumé, health records, information gathered about a particular job or career

* Indicates a form or forms provided in *The File-a-Plan* that you might use to record information in that category. Print a Category Reference Sheet (on the CD) for each category you wish to use. File it in front of the category for quick reference.

File-a-Plan Archive Category List

1. Attendance

2. Catalogs and Curriculum

3. Field Trips

4. Grades and Evaluation

5. Household

6. Lesson Plans

7. Medical and Health Records

8. Optional Study and Activities

9. Organizations

10. Portfolio and Sample Work

11. Potential Projects

12. Review

13. Testing

14. Transcripts

15. Work, Career, and College Planning

Refer to the Category Reference sheets for each category, found on the accompanying CD, to determine what to file, archive, and discard.

Visit the Web site at www.MarilynRockett.com. Copyright 1990–2007 Marilyn Rockett. Copy for personal use only.

File-a-Plan Form List: Descriptions

Each of these forms with instructions and helps are on the CD that accompanies this book. This list is an overview to aid you in deciding which forms may benefit you in your household and homeschool. You may copy forms and any information from the CD for your personal use only. Please abide by the letter and the spirit of the U.S. copyright laws, and do not copy and share the forms with others. Of course, I appreciate your recommendation of this book and CD to your friends.

No one will (or should) use all these forms. Choose those that apply to you and your family and help you accomplish your home and school tasks. The forms are listed alphabetically by title.

1. **Attendance Record**—Record attendance for those who must meet that requirement.
2. **Clean Room Chart**—A guide for your children's chores.
3. **Counting the Cost**—Track your education expenses.
4. **Curriculum Sources**—Record and/or compare curriculum materials.
5. **Daily Works**—Keep one day's plans for home and school on one page; effective for large families.
6. **Field Trip Minder**—Plan and/or research field trips. Useful for a family or for a support group leader to plan trips for a group.
7. **Goal Minder**—Keep goals for older students and adults.
8. **Grade or Goal Report**—Keep grades or record progress for a student.

9. **Health Record**—Keep health records for each family member.

10. **Help! Information I Need**—Keep vital information easily accessible.

11. **High School Plan**—Record an overall plan for older students.

12. **High School Transcript**—A transcript designed for homeschoolers.

13. **Home Works Planner**—Household evaluation sheet mentioned in chapter 2.

14. **Household Minder**—A chore chart for children who are readers.

15. **Individual Evaluation**—Clarify the needs of a family member old enough to understand and set goals.

16. **List Minder**—Make a list of any kind on this generic list form.

17. **Master Household Routine**—Form a framework for a simple household routine.

18. **Menu Minder**—Plan weekly menus that are adaptable.

19. **Mission Statement**—Record a personal and/or family mission statement.

20. **People and Resources**—Keep any type grouping of names, addresses, or information for a general address log or for a specific organization.

21. **Project or Idea Minder**—Plan a major project for family or for school.

22. **Reading and Library Minder**—Record books read, create a required reading list, keep a record of books loaned or borrowed, and record a list of books to buy or check out at the library.

23. **Standardized and Achievement Test Record**—Record test results and make notes that allow you to choose curriculum and evaluate your students.

24. **Student Assignments**—Allow older students to work independently yet still supervise their work.

25. **Student Contract**—Hold students accountable for work while they work independently.

26. **Study Plan**—Map a study path whether you use a traditional or less conventional method.

27. **Subject or Unit Worksheet**—Record details after planning a study path; compare to scope and sequence.

28. **Weakness and Strength Evaluation**—Evaluate each child for better training.

29. **Weekly Lesson Planner**—Record lesson plans in multiple ways on this form.

30. **Weekly Studies Log**—Record student lessons and activities with one page for a week.

31. **Weekly Works**—Track your week's to-do's.

32. **Weekly Works for Students**—Student version of a weekly to-do.

Available Seminars and Workshops

Marilyn offers encouragement to homeschoolers and Christian women in the vital areas of managing their households, educating their children, and relationships with others and the Lord. In the seminars/workshops, Marilyn amplifies some of the information in *Homeschooling at the Speed of Life*; she also covers topics that are not in the book.

For further information, contact her at Marilyn@MarilynRockett.com or visit the Web site at www.MarilynRockett.com.

Marilyn is available to present the following topics for your group or event. Check the Web site for updates and additions.

One-day Events

Passing the Baton is a fast-paced, multimedia seminar that equips today's Christian adults to have an eternal impact in the lives of tomorrow's culture-shaping leaders. Passing the Baton is a one-day seminar for homeschool groups or private schools. Don't miss this informative and practical experience.

You can also customize a one-day seminar by choosing up to six topics from the following list that fit your group's needs. The topics can be presented individually as well.

Individual Topics

- Foundation for Organization—A Walk Through the Word
- Finishing Well (workshop for leaders or a keynote address)
- Educating for Eternity (keynote address)
- Homeschooling at the Speed of Life
- Clutter, Clutter Everywhere and Not a Spot to Think
- Teaching Children Life Skills
- Paper by the Pile
- Linking the Generations through Home Education (workshop for grandparents or keynote address)
- PATHS for Life—Priorities and Goal Setting
- Special "Days" to Organize
- Home-taught Teens in the Real World

Notes

Chapter 1

1. Irish Proverb. Louise Bachelder, editor, *Little Things* (Mount Vernon, NY: The Peter Pauper Press, 1969), 46.

MARGIN QUOTATIONS

Steven Covey, http://quotations.about.com/cs/inspirationquotes (retrieved 07/01/2006).
Gordon McDonald, *Ordering Your Private World: Expanded Edition* (Nashville, Tenn.: Oliver Nelson, a division of Thomas Nelson, Inc., 1985), 12.
Benjamin Franklin, http://quotations.about.com/cs/inspirationquotes (retrieved 07/06/2006).
Richard A. Swenson, MD, *Margin* (Colorado Springs, Colo.: NavPress Publishing Group, 1992), 223.

Chapter 2

1. Daniel Webster. Bachelder, *Little Things*, 15.
2. Elisabeth Elliot, *Keep a Quiet Heart* (Grand Rapids, Mich.: Revell, division of Baker Publishing Group, 1995), 57.

MARGIN QUOTATIONS

Henry Ford, http://quoteworld.org/categories/time/2 (retrieved 07/08/2006).
Author Unknown, http://quotations.about.com/cs/inspirationquotes (retrieved 07/08/2006).
W. Clement Stone, www.wisdomquotes.com/cat_plans.html (retrieved 07/09/2006).
Stacy McDonald, *Raising Maidens of Virtue* (Barker, Tex.: Books on the Path, 2004), 49.

A. A. Milne (creator of Winnie the Pooh), http://en.thinkexist.com/quotes/a._a._milne/2.html (retrieved 07/16/2006).

John F. Kennedy, http://quotationspage.com/subjects/time (retrieved 07/08/2006).

Hugh Blair, "On the Importance of Order in Conduct," *Sermons*, Vol. 1, Num. 16, (1822), 195.

Charles Baudelaire. Bachelder, *Little Things*, 39.

Debbie Strayer, *Gaining Confidence to Teach* (Melrose, Fla.: Common Sense Press, 1997), 131.

Ibid., 5.

Josh Billings. Bachelder, *Little Things*, 39.

C. S. Lewis, www.wisdomquotes.com/cat_time.html (retrieved 07/12/2006).

Chapter 3
MARGIN QUOTATIONS

Milne, http://en.thinkexist.com/quotes/a._a._milne/2.html (retrieved 07/16/2006).

Old Chinese Proverb, http://en.thinkexist.com/quotations/planning/4.html (retrieved 07/08/2006).

Epictetus. Bachelder, *Little Things*, 15.

Chapter 4
MARGIN QUOTATIONS

Terry Dorian, and Zan Peters Tyler, *Anyone Can Homeschool* (Lafayette, La.: Huntington House Publishers, 1996), 170.

Leonardo Da Vinci, http://quotations.about.com/cs/inspirationquotes/a/Time1.htm (retrieved 07/08/2006).

Mark Twain. Bachelder, *Little Things*, 22.

Strayer, *Gaining Confidence to Teach*, 52.

Ibid., 134.

Ibid., 61.

Chapter 5
MARGIN QUOTATIONS

John Dryden. Bachelder, *Little Things*, 25.

Dorian, *Anyone Can Homeschool*, 171.

Chapter 6
MARGIN QUOTATIONS

Unknown author of proverb, http://en.thinkexist.com/quotations/planning (retrieved 07/17/2006).

Benjamin Franklin, www.wisdomquotes.com/cat_time.html (retrieved 07/08/2006).

Mary Ann Froehlich, *What's a Smart Woman Like You Doing In a Place Like This?* (Brentwood, Tenn.: Wolgemuth & Hyatt, 1989), 52.

Strayer, *Gaining Confidence to Teach*, 30.

Chapter 7

1. Ruth Beechick, *You Can Teach Your Child Successfully: Grades 4–8* (Pollock Pines, Calif.: Arrow Press, 1988), vii.

MARGIN QUOTATIONS:

Froehlich, *What's a Smart Woman Like You Doing In a Place Like This?*, 48.

Paul and Gena Suarez, general editors, *Homeschooling Methods* (Nashville, Tenn.: Broadman & Holman Publishers, 2006), 1.

Marilyn Rockett, quoted from numerous workshops.

Tyler, *Anyone Can Homeschool*, 33.

Chapter 8

1. Susan A. McDowell, "The Perceived Impact of Homeschooling on the Family in General and the Mother-Teacher in Particular," *Home School Researcher*, Vol. 13, No. 4; Vol. 14, No. 1, (1999), National Home Education Research Institute, www.nheri.org (retrieved 06/26/2006).

MARGIN QUOTATIONS

Henry Ward Beecher, http://en.thinkexist.com/quotes/with/keyword/schoolroom (retrieved 07/01/2006).

Edith Schaeffer, *What Is a Family?* (Old Tappan, NJ: Fleming H. Revell Co., 1975), 69.

Susan Schaeffer Macaulay, *For the Children's Sake* (Wheaton, Ill.: Crossway Books, 1984), 157.

Strayer, *Gaining Confidence to Teach*, 114.

Cathy Duffy, *100 Top Picks for Homeschool Curriculum* (Nashville, Tenn.: Broadman & Holman Publishers, 2005), 2.

Ruth Beechick, *Homeschooling Methods*, general editors: Paul and Gena Suarez (Nashville, Tenn.: Broadman & Holman Publishers, 2006), 229.

Chapter 9

1. Miller McPherson, Lynn Smith-Lovin, and Matthew E. Brashears. "Social isolation in America: Changes in core discussion networks over two decades." *American Sociological Review*, Vol. 71 (June 2006): 353–75 (retrieved 06/26/06). www.asanet.org/galleries/default-file/June06ASRFeature.pdf

MARGIN QUOTATIONS

Hagedorn. Bachelder, *Little Things*, 12.
Dorian, *Anyone Can Homeschool*, 169.
Schaeffer, *What Is a Family?*, 213.
McDonald. Bachelder, *Little Things*, 53.

Chapter 10

MARGIN QUOTATIONS

Dorian, *Anyone Can Homeschool*, 169.
Sally Clarkson, *Homeschooling Methods: Seasoned Advice on Learning Styles*, general editors: Paul and Gena Suarez (Nashville, Tenn.: Broadman & Holman Publishers, 2006), 256.
McDonald, *Ordering Your Private World: Expanded Edition*, 61.